New Directions for
Higher Education

Martin Kramer and
Judith Block McLaughlin
CO-EDITORS-IN-CHIEF

D1232856

Perspectives on Fundraising

J. Bradford Hodson
Bruce W. Speck
EDITORS

Number 149 • Spring 2010
Jossey-Bass
San Francisco

PERSPECTIVES ON FUNDRAISING
J. Bradford Hodson, Bruce W. Speck (eds.)
New Directions for Higher Education, no. 149
Martin Kramer, Judith Block McLaughlin, Co-Editors-in-Chief

Microfilm copies of issues and articles are available in 16mm and 35mm, as well as microfiche in 105mm, through University Microfilms Inc., 300 North Zeeb Road, Ann Arbor, MI 48106-1346.

NEW DIRECTIONS FOR HIGHER EDUCATION (ISSN 0271-0560, electronic ISSN 1536-0741) is part of The Jossey-Bass Higher and Adult Education Series and is published quarterly by Wiley Subscription Services, Inc., A Wiley Company, at Jossey-Bass, 989 Market Street, San Francisco, CA 94103-1741. Periodicals Postage Paid at San Francisco, California, and at additional mailing offices. POSTMASTER: Send address changes to New Directions for Higher Education, Jossey-Bass, 989 Market Street, San Francisco, CA 94103-1741.

New Directions for Higher Education is indexed in Current Index to Journals in Education (ERIC); Higher Education Abstracts.

SUBSCRIPTIONS cost $89 for individuals and $244 for institutions, agencies, and libraries. See ordering information page at end of journal.

EDITORIAL CORRESPONDENCE should be sent to the Co-Editors-in-Chief, Martin Kramer, 2807 Shasta Road, Berkeley, CA 94708-2011 and Judith Block McLaughlin, Harvard GSE, Gutman 435, Cambridge, MA 02138.

Cover photograph © Digital Vision

www.josseybass.com

CONTENTS

Editors' Notes

How do university leaders know if their institution's efforts to raise private gifts are effective? With so many presidents, provosts, and deans having very little hands-on experience in fundraising, that's often a difficult question to answer. What is not difficult is to see that the need for private gifts will only continue to escalate, particularly at public universities that have seen state investment in higher education deteriorate. Leaders of the academy are beginning to ask tough questions of their chief fundraising officers: "How can I integrate fundraising into the overall institutional message?" and "How do I know this is working?" Professional advancement staff, so often accustomed to making decisions with donors on the basis of gut instinct (fundraising is an art, not a science), are often unprepared to give specific answers, leaving the president or dean confused and frustrated.

Purpose of This Volume

The purpose of this issue of *New Directions for Higher Education* is to offer university administrators—presidents, provosts, academic deans, and others—some perspectives on fundraising that will assist them in building and assessing their institution's private giving operation. Fundraising is not difficult, but it does require discipline and an investment on the part of the institution. We say it's not difficult because when you boil fundraising down to its most basic element, it's simply a conversation between the institution and a person who has interest in the university and the financial capacity to make a gift. The effectiveness of the conversation hinges on the discipline to carry out the relationship consistently over a period of months or years, and on the commitment by the university to put staff and resources in the right place at the right time to increase the odds that the conversation will bear fruit. This is the essence of fundraising, and this volume expands on the conversation by giving university leaders nine perspectives on topical issues facing administrators desirous of raising private money more effectively.

Overview of the Book

Authors who have experience raising money in higher education have written the nine chapters of this volume. They offer their own unique perspectives on the practice of fundraising and the particular topic they address in their respective chapter. Topics were selected from discussion between

the editors as to what questions were on the minds of university leaders today regarding fundraising. The information contained in this volume is not intended to be highly theoretical, for two reasons: first, there is a paucity of empirical research available on fundraising; and second, the editors and authors intend for the information to be practicable and applicable. Readers should find immediate "take-aways" they can use to answer their own questions about fundraising.

Taken as a whole, this volume offers a great variety of information on topics of current interest to presidents, provosts, deans, and other leaders of the academy. For instance, one of the most vexing fundraising issues facing a president, particularly a president from a wholly academic background, is how to balance the fundraising needs of intercollegiate athletics with the fundraising needs of the academic community. Certainly, a university exists to educate students and foster academic research, but those areas can sometimes lack "sex appeal" for prospective donors. Intercollegiate athletics, by contrast, is laden with passion, excitement, competition, and donor/fan enthusiasm. Presidents often are torn between their desire to keep athletics healthy and competitive for the sake of increasing the visibility of the institution and the real financial needs of academic departments and programs. In the end, the donor will make the decision about where to invest his or her private gift, but the president has an opportunity to guide donor interest toward one area or another, or both. Maintaining this balance is tricky and can lead to criticism from the academic community on campus or the legion of sports fans off campus. It's practical issues of this type that this volume has attempted to address.

Overview of the Chapters

In Chapter One, "The Growing Role of Private Giving in Financing the Modern University," Bruce Speck outlines the sources of funding higher education and shares how private giving is reshaping the academy. In describing private philanthropy for scholarships, facilities, equipment, and faculty, he illustrates public higher education's increasing reliance on private support. This reliance, according to Speck, has fostered a new paradigm for financing the modern university and altered the way in which leaders in higher education view private philanthropy.

In Chapter Two, "The Foundation-Institution Partnership: The Role of Institutionally Related Foundations in Public Higher Education," David Bass recounts the origins of the institutionally related foundation and discusses the important role these organizations play in the success of a public university's fundraising program. Bass presents details about the types of institutionally related foundations and how elements such as a memorandum of understanding can help facilitate a successful relationship between the foundation and the college or university it was established to assist.

In Chapter Three, "The Challenge of Funding Fundraising," Robert Holmes explores the various methods of obtaining monies to finance the university's development operation. The adage that it takes money to make money has never been truer. Funding mechanisms Holmes explores include institutional support, unrestricted gifts, management fees, gift fees, temporary investment earnings, and revenue from real estate. Pros and cons for each method are explored, and Holmes breaks down the financial needs of start-up, growing, and mature fundraising operations.

In Chapter Four, "Leading the Way: The Role of Presidents and Academic Deans in Fundraising," Brad Hodson explores the specialized roles that the university president and deans of the institution's academic colleges play in the fundraising enterprise. Both the president and the dean have the responsibility for creating a compelling vision, setting organizational priorities, communicating the case for support, and engaging constituents. Hodson also discusses unique roles for these two leaders of the academy, among them assessing institutional readiness to raise funds, working with faculty, and engaging advisory boards. Special attention is given to the role of professional fundraising staff in supporting the fundraising roles of the president and the academic dean.

In Chapter Five, "Determining the Success of Fundraising Programs," Thomas Hiles explores how an institution can assess the return it receives on investment in the fundraising operation. What may surprise some is that determining success is much more than simply dollars raised. Hiles walks the reader through other metrics such as number of donor contacts, number of proposals presented and the percentage of those proposals accepted, and overcoming objections to the ask. Since fundraising operations are at differing stages of maturity, Hiles doesn't take a one-size-fits-all approach. Instead, he offers insight into measuring success in start-up programs and more mature fundraising operations alike.

In Chapter Six, "Integrating Development, Alumni Relations, and Marketing for Fundraising Success," Thomas Stevick presents a model for bringing together the advancement functions of fundraising, alumni and constituent relations, and public relations and marketing. Although these three areas are often housed in the same organizational unit (often called "university advancement"), they are sometimes siloed in their approaches to supporting fundraising. Stevick proposes that the push for integration starts at the top with the vice president and president. He also offers what he refers to as the "corporate model" whereby sales and marketing are integrated in public companies and both are focused on revenue generation. Finally, Stevick lays out a four-step plan for bringing fundraising, alumni relations, and marketing together and focusing their efforts on a single message and end result.

In Chapter Seven, "Balancing Fundraising in Academic Programs and Intercollegiate Athletics," authors Elizabeth King, Eric Sexton, and James

Rhatigan begin by labeling as "uneasy" the relationship between fundraising for academic programs and athletics. But the authors don't allow the label to become a foregone conclusion. Instead, King, Sexton, and Rhatigan offer two practical models—centralized and decentralized fundraising operations—as alternatives to ease the fundraising tension between the academy and athletics. The authors then explore best practices from across the country, highlighting examples of intercollegiate athletic organizations being an asset to fundraising for the academy rather than a distraction. This chapter takes a fresh perspective on an issue that has vexed institutional leaders since the day private giving became central to the funding of higher education rather than just a sideline enterprise.

In Chapter Eight, "Prospect Development Systems: Empowering Artful Fundraising," Dan Nicoson answers the question, "How do you move someone from being a suspect to becoming a prospect?" Institutional leaders with little fundraising experience can often be unrealistic about the methodical way individuals, corporations, and foundations move from being just one of many with interest in the university to becoming a donor that actually invests in the institution. As Nicoson explains, movement through the pipeline often takes months and years as well as many personal, focused visits between the prospect and a representative of the university. Much work goes into determining if a potential donor has the interest in the institution and the capacity to make a gift. Prospect screening, research, peer evaluation, and development of a cultivation strategy are all areas Nicoson explores as he describes how the university moves someone who was once just a person among thousands to the point where he or she is in a position to close a philanthropic gift.

In Chapter Nine, "Recruiting, Training, and Retaining High-Performance Development Teams," Stephen Elder offers insight into how institutions identify and develop the talents of professional fundraising staff. Fundraising is an art, not a science, and much of the work done by major gift officers is intuitive in nature. Because of this, good fundraisers are great relationship builders. Sustaining those relationships is to the benefit of both the donor and the institution. Therefore, as Elder points out, retaining good fundraisers is of the utmost importance to universities that want to maximize their fundraising potential. Elder spends considerable time discussing retention strategies such as being clear about expectations, giving the officers responsibilities they can call their own, and creating an environment that fosters mutual trust and feedback. Given the amount of time and money universities invest in getting major gift officers out into the field and making them effective, retention is simply protecting the institution's investment and enhancing the likelihood of future fundraising success.

Conclusion

A full exploration of all of the current fundraising topics in American higher education would be overwhelming. Instead, we have tried to give the reader a broad look at some of the most timely and important issues facing university presidents, academic deans, and other institutional leaders as they work to increase private gifts flowing into the organization. We hope this volume will encourage university leaders to become more actively engaged in fundraising, both as an administrator and as a participant. For those who already consider themselves to be active fundraisers, we hope this volume furnishes information that will allow thinking more deeply about the impact of philanthropy on campus and their role in fostering success in private giving. For all institutions, we wish great success in this growing area of financial importance. No institution in America will be left unaffected by private gifts. Becoming knowledgeable about how to maximize an institution's potential in this area is of the first priority for current and future university leaders.

J. Bradford Hodson
Bruce W. Speck
Editors

J. BRADFORD HODSON is the vice president for university advancement at Pittsburg State University and executive director of the PSU Foundation.

BRUCE W. SPECK is president of Missouri Southern State University in Joplin.

1

Increased use of private funds to support public higher educa-
tion is essential, but private funding undoubtedly shapes the
university in ways that challenge academic traditions, creat-
ing a new paradigm for financing the modern university.

The Growing Role of Private Giving in Financing the Modern University

Bruce W. Speck

Imagine working for an employer your entire career and finding that your starting salary was the highest you ever earned. Virtually every year, your salary decreased, until, at the end of a long career, you retire earning less money than you did during your first year of employment. Those who have worked in state-supported institutions of higher education during the last twenty years don't have to use their imagination to envision the steady and precipitous decline in state appropriations that currently are at an all-time low. As Zumeta (2004) says:

> State support for higher education—which includes core operating support for public institutions, a total of some $5 billion annually in state funding for student scholarships and grants, direct aid to private colleges and universities in some states, and funding for state governance operations—has fallen steadily as a percentage of personal income across all fifty states for more than twenty years. . . . Even counting tuition revenue, which has been growing rapidly, total funding for higher education per student has increased only sluggishly since the mid-1980s [p. 83].

Therefore, Hossler notes, "Many institutions have started to describe themselves as state-assisted rather than state-supported" (2004, p. 150). In fact, some would say public higher education has moved from the status of state-assisted to merely being state-located. Why state support for higher education has dwindled at an alarming rate is a source of debate (Alfred, 1996;

NEW DIRECTIONS FOR HIGHER EDUCATION, no. 149, Spring 2010 © Wiley Periodicals, Inc.
Published online in Wiley InterScience (www.interscience.wiley.com) • DOI: 10.1002/he.376

Thelin, 2004, 2009). But a monumental shift in funding for higher education has occurred nationwide.

Take, for example, California. Yudof (2009), in capsule form, offers a glimpse of the national problem as it is manifested in California.

> In the 1980s, for example, higher education made up 17 percent of the state budget, and prisons accounted for 3 percent. Today those figures are 9 percent and 10 percent. Students, by and large, have been forced to pick up the difference because, when it comes to our core support, we have only two main sources: taxpayer dollars from the state and student tuition. When one decreases, the other almost inevitably must go up by an equal measure. In effect, while the state once provided a freeway to higher education, it can now only offer a toll road, with students paying more and more of the cost [p. A31].

In acknowledging that public funding for higher education has declined, McKeown (1996) posits the need to view a method for funding higher education that is enmeshed in a political process involving compromise: "Compromise will be necessary to preserve and improve the quality of public higher education and to accommodate the changing conditions of education in the new millennium." Then McKeown asks a haunting question about reaching the lofty goal of quality and access as a social contract or governmental promise to its citizens: "Perhaps the promise will never be fulfilled, not because the goals were unworthy but because the goals have changed. Or, has the promise changed?" (pp. 84–85).

I assert that the promise of high-quality public education for everyone has changed, and I agree with McKeown when she says that the challenge before us is to develop "a new paradigm for higher education funding" (1996, p. 84). I am not optimistic that the new paradigm will include increased state support for higher education. In fact, it's reasonable to think that the current global economic crisis, a recession that has been compared to the Great Depression, coupled with the federal bailout funds to the states, will fundamentally change higher education in ways yet to be seen. A new paradigm for higher education, I predict, will emerge from the shattered economy, and this new paradigm, whatever its final form, will include a renewed focus on increased private funding for public higher education because state support will not rise appreciably. But before I discuss the growing role of eleemosynary giving in funding the restructured university, I think it is useful to describe the current sources of funding for higher education, in part because there is often confusion about the economics of higher education.

Sources for Funding Higher Education

Up to this point, I have focused on state appropriations for higher education, but *in toto* budgets for higher education are composed of three other sources of funding: tuition and fees; grants, particularly for sponsored research; and funds raised through charitable donations.

Tuition and Fees. First, and foremost, is state appropriations coupled with tuition and fees. I collapse state appropriations into tuition and fees because the two are inextricably linked. As Yudof noted, "When one decreases the other must inevitably go up by an equal measure" (2009, p. A31). Indeed, fees are often not discussed openly when debate rages about the reasons for increased tuition, but fees have become a significant addendum to tuition, often as a way to limit tuition increases. At one campus where I worked, all students were charged a "campus access fee." A parking permit was issued in response to paying this mandatory fee. However, even if students did not own or drive a car on campus, they were required to pay the fee. An access fee by another name would be called a parking fee, but the virtue of a mandatory "access" fee for every student is that it brings in more revenue than a parking fee for just some students, and the moniker *access* is vague enough to cover a multitude of "access" issues.

In any particular year, when the state decreases funding for higher education by giving less than is needed to keep up with increasing costs, tuition and fees have been increased to help make up for the shortfall. *Help* is an important qualifier. Even though the outcry about astronomical increases in tuition and fees goes unabated, in fact tuition and fees, though indeed they have increased beyond the Consumer Price Index (CPI) during the last decades, have not filled the gap left by ever-dwindling state funds to higher education. In addition, increases in tuition and fees can have a counterproductive effect. The higher the tuition and fees, the greater the probability that enrollment will decrease because a portion of the students can no longer afford to pay the price of attendance.

Grants. The second source of revenue is grants, particularly sponsored research, and especially for research universities, but even in limited ways for comprehensive universities and community colleges. The term *sponsored research* includes federal government monies for TRIO programs, state grants, grants from foundations, and the like. Grants work well for research universities because the tremendous infrastructure needed to support heavy involvement and success in grantsmanship can pay dividends when researchers secure federal dollars and build their reputation to keep the research cycle going by winning more grants, which furnish further evidence that federal money is being spent productively, so that yet another grant can be secured.

Grant funding is also valuable for the university because of overhead costs. Most grants allow a certain percentage of overhead costs to be recouped by the sponsoring institution, and those overhead costs are helpful in replacing operating budget dollars that can now be used elsewhere. In addition, grants also allow grantees to hire people, buy goods and services, and generally stimulate the university economy. Alas, grants are highly competitive (Hossler, 2004) and friable. Misconduct in research undertaken with the aid of federal grants can create havoc for an entire institution. The shifting fortunes of the federal dollar and the morphing of federal policies regarding research priorities can have a deleterious impact on one sort of lab and an entrepreneurial impact on another sort. At any rate, federal grant dollars are a significant source of income for research universities, and nonresearch grants (such as those competitive grants for TRIO programs) can benefit all colleges and universities, but for the most part federal grants based on research productivity are designed for institutions that produce doctoral students in the sciences.

Charitable Donations. The third source of funds, as discussed later, is raised through charitable donations, acquiring extramural support.

That's it.

There are no other sources of funding for higher education. Endowment income and enterprise income from properties treated as endowment are really only charitable contributions in another guise. And when the gap in funding widens between what is realistically needed to supply quality education and what the state allocates (plus tuition and fees), resources from the other two sources are used to help narrow the gap.

The third source of funding is my focus for the rest of this chapter because fundraising has become the *sine qua non* for all public universities. However, mine is a cautionary tale about the essential need to secure private funding for public higher education. I begin the tale with the benefits of extramural funding, but I end with painful realities about the limits of fundraising and possible implications for the academy as a whole when private money becomes critical to maintain public higher education.

The Value of Fundraising

The gap in funding that has been created "because the state is no longer a reliable partner" (Yudof, 2009, p. A31) is probably impossible to span by appealing for more state support, but fundraising can help span the gap in significant ways: by funding facilities and scholarships, and by furnishing undesignated funds.

Facilities. How do institutions of higher education acquire funds for new facilities? The state can appropriate funds, but as we have seen the state has had difficulty in allocating sufficient operating funds, much less resources for new facilities. (Or, more to the point, the state has had difficulty furnishing resources for maintenance and repair of existing facilities.) Nevertheless, states have either appropriated dollars for buildings or issued bonds for capital projects. Because capital projects for state universities are often prioritized (or based on political maneuvering—or both) and because state funding for capital projects is severely limited, it can take a decade or more to honor requests for new facilities. The process for seeking state support for a new building can often be moved along if a donor can supply a portion of the cost for the desired facility. Some states give preference to capital projects that have matching funds from a private donor, often accompanied by naming rights. The needed building will be named for the donor, and the state partners with a private citizen to erect a new facility.

The naming of a building is certainly an advantageous method of getting new construction approved, but the naming of a school is an even bigger boon to a campus. The name for a building is generally calculated anywhere from 10 to 50 percent of the cost to construct the building. The name of a school, however, can be valued at twice the annual operating budget of the school.

The use of fees to support all manner of needs on campus is another opportunity to solicit private donations, even for buildings. Perhaps one of the most familiar projects in the modern academy that relies on student fees is the obligatory recreation center. Student fees are assessed, generally by the students themselves through the student senate, to fund a recreation center. However, naming rights for a recreation center allow the president to enhance the center.

A building can be an exciting addition to a campus, generating enthusiasm for the university, pride in the *alma mater*, and desire to attend on the part of prospective students. However, buildings require upkeep, and unless the occupants of a building generate sufficient income to offset operating costs, or the naming of a building generates sufficient revenue (as in an endowment) to fund the operating costs, the university's operating budget will be used for new costs associated with maintaining a new building—perpetually. As a footnote, most states do not include continuing funds for operating a building, so when the state funds a new building, in whole or in part, operating costs are not included.

Scholarships. Because the costs of higher education have steadily increased, often outpacing the CPI, university presidents seek ways to offset rising tuition costs by soliciting funds from private sources to award student scholarships. Of course, the absolutely best way to offer scholarships is through private endowments. Let's say a donor gives $1 million for scholarships. Once endowed—often after one year—the corpus will yield about 7 percent earnings under normal circumstances, or about $70,000. But to account for dips in the market, a prudent vice president for development, at the direction of the foundation board, will allocate 5 percent, or $50,000, to fund scholarships, keeping back 2 percent for fluctuations in the market. Making a scholarship commitment for four years that is based on students meeting particular requirements to keep the scholarship means making a multiyear commitment without knowing what the market will yield in years two, three, and four of the commitment.

If the donor specifies particular requirements for the endowed scholarship (say, must be awarded equally to five business students majoring in finance who graduated from Sudwig County with a GPA of at least 3.2), the money may or may not be awarded completely. If, however, the donor does not specify particular requirements, the earnings from the corpus can be

NEW DIRECTIONS FOR HIGHER EDUCATION • DOI: 10.1002/he

used in a variety of cases to help satisfy students' financial needs. In fact, undesignated scholarship funds can replace institutional resources that are used to discount tuition, freeing up operating funds for other pressing needs. However, I may be a bit hasty in replacing operating funds in the form of institutional scholarships with the earnings from a donor's corpus. The corpus will not grow, so the earnings, at 7 percent, will continue to yield the same amount of money. As tuition increases, many (not all) scholarships are adjusted upward to pay for increases in tuition or a percentage thereof. In a steady state of 7 percent earnings, the scholarship will remain fixed but tuition will undoubtedly increase, making the scholarship less valuable economically over time. Either the number or the amount of scholarships declines or else the operating budget can be tapped to make up the difference between increases in tuition and steady-state interest returns.

In fact, any endowment that is used to start a scholarship or program—if the corpus of the endowment is never increased—will eventually require other sources of funding to support the scholarship or program as the costs of education increase. Take, for example, an endowment that yielded $200,000 twenty years ago and was used to start an honors program. Initially, the earnings from the corpus yielded a happy surplus because the first class of honor students is guaranteed a four-year scholarship. Then the second-year students are likewise guaranteed a four-year scholarship. Attrition in the honors program is quite low, so the four-year guarantees begin committing much of the $200,000, until all four classes of the undergraduate honor students are fully funded. (We haven't even added operating expenses for the program.) Twenty years later, tuition has increased substantially through a series of yearly increases, and the $200,000 is no longer adequate to support the four-year cycle of scholarships. Likely, university operating funds will be tapped to bridge the gap between commitments and the available funds for the scholarships, and this gap will be filled by the university operating budget unless an ongoing effort has been made to acquire other funds for the honor students' scholarships. In short, what was hailed as an important gift in establishing a program loses its economic luster over time. (Throughout the twenty years, the program's operating budget has been increased, even if only meagerly.) In fact, such gifts can become a liability because the university operating budget is tapped to support a program that did not foresee the need for ongoing funding to support a worthy cause.

Undesignated Funds. Perhaps the most delicious donations come from donors who simply say, "Here's my gift. Use it as you see fit." Those funds—unrestricted by specific requirements for their use—allow a president flexibility in funding various projects. Such funds can be used as seed money for a project or as supplements for pressing needs or new opportunities that require one-time funds. However, typically a donor who makes a significant investment in the university wants a significant say in how the money is used—sometimes down to the color of carpet or the design of a new stadium.

The Cautionary Part of the Tale

I have already noted various cautions related to acquiring external private funding—the problem of maintaining and repairing a building named after a generous donor, the need to think providentially about supplementing the earnings from a corpus to maintain ongoing scholarships and programs, the difficulty of securing unrestricted funds to prime other projects or fill gaps in revenues—and a theme emerges from those cautions: the operating budget can be strained over time as the normal costs of maintenance are incurred or the increasing costs of keeping a commitment outpace the earnings from a corpus. Therefore, fundraising becomes a self-perpetuating activity, and I have not even discussed all manner of stuff that is part of the arms race in higher education—Jumbotrons, scientific gadgets for laboratories, bigger and better athletic facilities, computers and all that is required to support them, electronic resources for libraries, and so on. Fundraising is essential, but as with all things human, fundraising is not the panacea for the states' historical and ongoing practice of reducing funding to state institutions of higher education. Fundraising supplements what has not been given, but at this point in time resources garnered through fundraising have supplanted needed state appropriations, and by supplanting state appropriations private funds must be given greater consideration in how higher education operates.

Conclusion

I return to the need for a new paradigm for funding public higher education. I do not pretend to sketch the paradigm, but I have shown that private funding to support public higher education will be essential. The new paradigm will undoubtedly have significant implications for higher education, and I pose a series of questions to suggest what some of the implications will be.

The Role of the State. At present, state-assisted (or state-located) institutions of higher education are governed by an array of state rules and regulations because states furnish taxpayer dollars to support higher education. Those rules and regulations can be a disservice to institutions that seek enrollment, partnership, and programmatic opportunities that are currently disallowed or heavily encumbered by state laws. For example, in many states for a university to develop a new degree program it must cut a significant yardage of red tape, an exercise in scissorship that private institutions can often avoid because they are not receiving state dollars (or in some cases, not many state dollars). Consequently, privates have a competitive advantage. Because states are unable or unwilling to support public higher education, should a new calculus be devised that relaxes the bureaucratic grip on universities so that they too can be competitive with privates? If states do not develop a new calculus but persist in asserting, regardless of their share of stock in higher education, that they have a duty to protect taxpayer dollars regardless of the proportionate benefit the dollars accrue, it seems reasonable to foresee a continuing competitive disadvantage for public institutions of higher education, perpetuating a downward economic spiral.

Indeed, although I have focused on public higher education to the exclusion of community colleges, I would be remiss if I did not point out the huge economic benefit in terms of low tuition students receive by attending a community college. As community colleges become even more attractive because of their tuition vis-à-vis universities, it is not hard to imagine that universities may be transformed into upper-division and graduate institutions, increasing the need for raising external funds for scholarships and fellowships.

A Business Model for the University. Academics are often offended when the university is discussed in terms of a business model. The concept of the corporate world as typified by the term *business model* is distasteful to them because academia is embodied in the world of ideals, which should not be sullied by talk of business. The mismatch between the reality of essential business functions a university performs and their relationship to academics is in and of itself a major problem when economics is such a powerful driver that is transforming *how* the university operates. Increased use of private funds to fuel the university's economy, therefore, raises various questions about university operating budgets. I focus on what I perceive is a major economic issue related to the essence of higher education: What price quality?

We use the term *quality education* as though it is a monolithic term. It isn't. Just as a person can purchase either a quality Ford Taurus or a quality Mercedes-Benz, students can purchase a specific type of quality education. Is it not naïve to think that a certain level of quality does not have a price tag? Isn't quality defined in relationship to the make and model of the university? Shirvani (2009) raises questions about the price of status in higher education, which is linked with the larger question of quality.

Talking about quality in the abstract is not a productive approach to determining how quality is defined at a particular institution, and the definition, if honesty be told, will have quantitative (including an economic price tag) and qualitative measures. Unfortunately, some in the academy have often dismissed quality issues related to economics.

The President's Role. I recently heard a candidate for an academic administrative job say, "A president's role is to bring in the money; a provost's role is to spend the money." Of course, such a view is naïve at best, and dangerously misleading at worst, as if a provost controlled the entire university budget. However, the part about the president's role raises questions about the qualifications for presidents as fundraising takes on an ever-larger part of presidential duties. To what extent do presidents need to be academics? Why not limit presidential duties regarding academics and let the vice president for academic affairs handle almost entirely the academic side of the house? Should university presidents in the new economy be required to pass some sort of litmus test regarding fundraising skills, if fundraising is a vital part of presidential duties? (Why wouldn't vice presidents for development make ideal presidential candidates?) Could it be that presidents will no longer be required to have earned a doctorate—or have earned a yet-to-be developed doctorate in presidential duties?

The Faculty's Role. Perhaps imperceptibly, but with growing angst, faculty perceive that their role has changed as the economic realities of higher education make budget tightening a reality. As the idealism of the life of the mind is challenged by the bottom line, faculty discontent is aroused, especially regarding tenure as embodied in tenure and tenure-track positions and shared governance. The elephant in the room is tenure, and there may be no gingerly way to ask whether we can afford to maintain a tenure system that does not support agility in a fluctuating labor market apparently demanding programmatic changes in a short time. This question is important because the largest percentage of the budget of any state-supported institution of higher education is dedicated to salaries and benefits (Chronister, 1996). Fukuyama (2009) believes, "The freedom guaranteed by tenure is precious. But it's time to abolish this institution before it becomes too costly, both financially and intellectually." Will the sheer weight of economic necessity outweigh arguments about the "preciousness" of tenure? If so, will labor unions have an increasingly important role in organizing faculty labor on behalf of an old paradigm of work that appears to be at odds with the modern academy? Will shared governance be transformed so that decisions about how the academy operates are less driven by governance models that require faculty, staff, and students to have a voice in how the university operates?

In addition, tenure is solidly welded to shared governance. This does not necessarily need to be the operational paradigm regarding shared governance. Like staff, faculty can be engaged in decisions about how the university functions, without the benefit of tenure. Clearly, however, the role of faculty in shared governance would change, because without tenure faculty members would have to adopt a new approach to shared governance that would likely require a more tempered and nuanced view of their other colleagues on campus (staff and administrators). In most cases, this new view would entail a greater focus on teamwork and the corporate good.

If it is the case that the person who holds the purse strings determines how resources are spent, what will increased reliance on private donors yield regarding how public higher education is shaped? I have suggested possible changes the academy might be faced with as public institutions of higher education rely more and more on private funding. However, whether my suggested changes come to fruition is not the major point. What is irrefutable is the fact that increased private investment in public higher education will change the academy because donors give to promote their vision of the academy, and if their vision matches existing needs as the university sees those needs, so much the better. If not, we'll take their money and adjust our vision to theirs—which we already do.

References

Alfred, R. L. "Competition for Limited Resources: Realities, Prospects, and Strategies." In D. S. Honeyman, J. L. Wattenbarger, and K. C. Westbrook (eds.), *A Struggle to Survive: Funding Higher Education in the Next Century*. Thousand Oaks, Calif.: Corwin Press, 1996.

Chronister, J. L. "Benefit and Retirement Issues in Higher Education." In D. S. Honeyman, J. L. Wattenbarger, and K. C. Westbrook (eds.), *A Struggle to Survive: Funding Higher Education in the Next Century*. Thousand Oaks, Calif.: Corwin Press, 1996.

Fukuyama, F. "Why We Should Get Rid of Tenure," 2009. Retrieved Apr. 21, 2009, from http://www.washingtonpost.com/wp-dyn/content/article/2009/04/16/AR2009041603466.html.

Hossler, D. "Refinancing Public Universities: Student Enrollments, Incentive-Based Budgeting, and Incremental Revenue." In E. P. St. John and M. D. Parsons (eds.), *Public Funding of Higher Education: Changing Contexts and New Rationales*. Baltimore: Johns Hopkins University Press, 2004, pp. 145–163.

McKeown, M. P. "State Funding Formulas: Promise Fulfilled?" In D. S. Honeyman, J. L. Wattenbarger, and K. C. Westbrook (eds.), *A Struggle to Survive: Funding Higher Education in the Next Century*. Thousand Oaks, Calif.: Corwin Press, 1996, pp. 49–85.

Shirvani, H. "Will a Culture of Entitlement Bankrupt Higher Education?" *Chronicle of Higher Education*, Oct. 23, 2009, p. A96.

Thelin, J. R. "Higher Education and the Public Trough: A Historical Perspective." In E. P. St. John and M. D. Parsons (eds.), *Public Funding of Higher Education: Changing Contexts and New Rationales*. Baltimore: Johns Hopkins University Press, 2004.

Thelin, J. R. "How to Bail out Public Universities." *Chronicle of Higher Education*, Oct. 23, 2009, p. A35.

Yudof, M. G. "From a President: We Will Not Surrender to Mediocrity." *Chronicle of Higher Education*, Oct. 9, 2009, p. A31.

Zumeta, W. "State Higher Education Financing: Demand Imperatives Meet Structural, Cyclical, and Political Constraints." In E. P. St. John and M. D. Parsons (eds.), *Public Funding of Higher Education: Changing Contexts and New Rationales*. Baltimore: Johns Hopkins University Press, 2004, pp. 79–107.

Bruce W. Speck *is president of Missouri Southern State University in Joplin.*

2

Institutionally related foundations play an important role in helping public colleges and universities realize their aspirations to receive private philanthropic dollars. This chapter contains practical advice for maintaining a successful foundation and fostering a positive relationship between that organization and its host institution.

The Foundation-Institution Partnership: The Role of Institutionally Related Foundations in Public Higher Education

David Bass

Institutionally related foundations have played a vital role in raising and managing private resources in support of public institutions of higher education. Unlike private grant-making foundations, college and university foundations are typically incorporated as public charities under section 501(c)(3) of the Internal Revenue Code. Although they may perform a range of functions, the primary purpose of most college and university foundations is to help raise private support for their affiliated institution or system, and hold and manage contributed assets. Many foundations were originally established to receive and steward private gifts, help segregate private and public funds, manage endowments, and facilitate financial transactions or entrepreneurial ventures that could not be undertaken effectively by state entities. The Kansas University (KU) Endowment Association, for example, was founded in 1891 to enable the university to use private gift funds to purchase a desirable parcel of land being offered to it at half its assessed value. The state constitution required that all gifts made to state institutions be deposited in a state-held general fund. As a private nonprofit corporation, the KU Endowment Association could accept private gift funds and purchase the real estate, which became part of the campus. Today more than two-thirds of the buildings at the University of Kansas were funded or furnished by the foundation, which has also allocated $587 million in support

New Directions for Higher Education, no. 149, Spring 2010 © Wiley Periodicals, Inc.
Published online in Wiley InterScience (www.interscience.wiley.com) • DOI: 10.1002/he.377

for students, faculty, programs, research, and capital projects over the past five years (KU Endowment, 2009). Even though the KU Endowment is generally recognized as the first institutionally related foundation, the vast majority of public institutions have established one or more such affiliated organizations.

The Need for Institutionally Related Foundations

Through the 1960s most public institutions had neither the ability nor the need to seek significant private support, receiving around 80 percent of their operating budgets from states. However, in 1977 public institutions received just 25 percent of all private support for higher education. Public institutions' share of private support climbed to 34 percent in 1987 and 42 percent in 1997. By 2007 public institutions raised 46 percent of all private support to higher education (Council for Aid to Education, n.d.). To offset losses in state appropriations, starting with the first major campaigns conducted by public institutions in the 1970s, fundraising in public higher education has grown exponentially, supported by establishment of new foundations and transformation of formerly passive "shell" foundations into organizations that have played a leading role in fundraising efforts.

The ability to engage committed, affluent, influential, and independent volunteer leaders is perhaps the most important way institutionally related foundations contribute to public institutions' fundraising. A 1987 survey of college and university fundraising practices found that 90 percent of single campus institutions have at least one affiliated foundation involved in fundraising. Further, 68 percent of public institutions regularly use foundation board members in fundraising activities, while just 39 percent use institution governing board members (Pocock, 1989).

The distinction between foundation boards and governing boards regarding fundraising is important. Public institution presidents and trustees have historically played a smaller role in fundraising than their counterparts at private institutions. About 70 percent of two-year institution boards and 90 percent of four-year and system boards of public institutions are appointed by governors or legislatures or are popularly elected (Schwartz and Akins, 2004). The political appointment process may preclude institutions from cultivating and recruiting institutional trustees with the specific experience, financial capacity, and personal and professional connections to serve as effective fundraisers. A 1997 survey on comprehensive campaigns underscores the leadership role played by foundation boards in public higher education fundraising, as well as the direct financial contributions they make. Of 198 public institutions, 88 percent reported having a separately incorporated foundation. Foundation board members were twice as likely to make campaign contributions as governing board members; 39 percent of foundation board members made campaign contributions or were expected to do so, while 19 percent of governing board members made or were expected to make campaign contributions. Foundation board members contributed 21 percent of the amount raised during the quiet phase of campaigns, compared to 4 percent contributed by institutional governing board members. On average, 34 percent of special campaign committee members were recruited from foundation boards; the figure is 7 percent drawn from institutional boards. Three-fourths of institutions asked foundation board members to make annual fund contributions, while 52 percent asked governing board members to do so (Schrum, 2000). The differing level of engagement in fundraising between public and private governing board members is borne out in the level of giving. In 2008, contributions from governing board members of private institutions accounted for 23 percent of the total funds contributed by individuals, while contributions from public institution governing board members accounted for 11 percent of funds raised from individuals (Kaplan, 2009).

In addition to fundraising support, foundation boards may play an important role in management of long-term investments and endowments and stewardship of privately contributed resources. Foundations can recruit board or investment committee members with the highly specialized investment expertise necessary to inspire donor confidence, and since foundation board members are typically among an institution's largest donors they are well equipped to serve as stewards of donors' private contributions. Although institutional governing boards must focus on annual budget cycles and are subject to continuous pressure from both internal and external stakeholders, foundation boards may be better equipped to maintain the long-term perspective essential to endowment management and the building of fundraising capacity. Finally, a self-perpetuating foundation board can strategically cultivate and recruit prospective board members with the specific skills and capacities best suited to the current and future leadership needs of the organization.

Practices to Mitigate Potential Foundation-Institution Conflict

As foundations assume a more active role in fundraising and supply leadership for other institutional priorities, such as real estate development, tensions can develop between institution and foundation boards and between the institution and the foundation. Growth in foundation assets; the increasing importance of private resources to public institutions' students, faculty, programs, and facilities; heightened standards of accountability; retirement of long-serving institutional and foundation presidents; and more "entrepreneurial" donors and board members can all raise the risk of foundation-institution conflict (Bass and Lanier, 2008).

Lack of clarity about the respective roles, prerogatives, and responsibilities of governing and foundation boards is perhaps the most fundamental source of conflict. As suggested earlier, foundation board members are likely to play an important leadership role in fundraising and make significant financial contributions to the institution; they often represent different constituents than appointed governing board members do. Differences in perspective, distrust of motives, disagreement about institutional priorities, and financial disputes can all undermine the relationships between foundation and institution boards.

A thoughtfully developed operating agreement or memorandum of understanding can help avoid such difficulties by clearly articulating the relationship between the foundation and institution and by outlining the respective responsibilities and mutual expectations of institution and foundation presidents and of institution governing and foundation boards. Such an operating agreement also specifies how funds are transferred between the foundation and institution, policies for sharing donor and alumni records, the foundation's administrative structure and funding, and other elements of the relationship. The process of developing the operating agreement is as important as the final agreement; it is an opportunity for institution and foundation presidents and boards to work closely together and establish a shared understanding about their respective responsibilities, roles, and obligations. The operating agreement should be periodically revisited to engage current staff and volunteer leaders in the process and ensure that the document reflects any changes in structure or roles. The Association of Governing Boards of Universities and Colleges and the Council for Advancement and Support of Education developed an illustrative memorandum of understanding outlining key principles and elements to bear in mind when negotiating an agreement (Legon, 2005).

The memorandum of understanding is particularly important in addressing issues in relation to compensation. For example, use of private resources to supplement the compensation of institution presidents, coaches, and other institution staff has proven a lightning rod for criticism, as have expenditures for presidential residences, travel, entertaining, and donor cultivation. In the illustrative memorandum of understanding cited just above, AGB and CASE encouraged "governing boards to assume full responsibility for providing for the compensation of institution leaders. When private support is necessary, institutions and foundations should structure such supplements in ways that limit the foundation's influence in presidential selection and oversight" (Association of Governing Boards of Universities and Colleges, 2005).

Regardless of how foundation-institution relationships are formally structured, candid communication and collaboration among foundation and institution leaders is essential. Some foundation bylaws stipulate that the institution president or a current governing board member must serve as an ex-officio member of the foundation board. This can enhance two-way communication and help ensure that the foundation board is fully apprised of the institution's strategic priorities. Appointing appropriately qualified former governing board members to the foundation board can also greatly enhance communication. Although much of the work of public institutions' governing boards is subject to state freedom-of-information and open-meeting laws, foundations should strive to operate with the highest degree of transparency compatible with safeguarding donor privacy along with essential business information. Establishing a joint planning committee comprising the institution president, foundation chief executive, and chairs of both boards as well as their development committees further enhances collaboration and communication. As Gerald Fischer, former CEO of the University of Minnesota Foundation, has observed in personal communication with the author, commitment to full transparency and candor in communications between the institution president and the foundation executive and to a mutual policy of "no surprises" informs the effectiveness of more formal modes of communication and collaboration.

Close, collaborative, and trusting relationships between institution and foundation staff members are vital to a foundation-institution partnership, but recent audits of foundation-institution relationships underscore the importance of recognizing the separate corporate status of foundations and developing policies to reflect it. In a 2005 report, the Colorado State auditor suggested that "the complexity of the flow of money (between the University of Colorado and its foundation), combined with inadequate contracts governing the relationship between the two entities, reduces accountability for and transparency of expenditures" (2005, p. 5). The report enumerated various ways in which the two entities could clarify and formalize their relationship and enhance financial transparency and accountability. In addition, an April 2009 report to the Kansas Board of Regents outlined a number of problematic financial transactions and potential conflicts of interests stemming from informal relationships among employees of Kansas State University and affiliated organizations. The report concluded that

> although Kansas State University is affiliated with several entities with a common goal, the support and advancement of the University, many of these affiliated entities are separate legal entities unto themselves. As such, each entity should conduct its activities and pursue its mission cognizant of the need for clear lines of delineation which require a degree of structure, formality and transparency [Grant Thornton, 2009, p. 34].

The principles informing these reports can go a long way toward precluding problems associated with use of foundation funds to compensate institution staff and support development activities.

As noted earlier, foundations commonly supplement the compensation of the institution's chief executive, but such supplements should be structured to ensure that the institution board retains full responsibility for selection, oversight, and compensation of the president, as well as to avoid the possibility of donor influence. Similarly, foundations may want to transfer funds designated for university development expenses to university accounts subject to institutional guidelines and oversight, rather than reimburse institution staff or pay vendors directly from foundation accounts. This can help the foundation avoid appearing to be a "slush fund" for inappropriate expenditures or personal benefit. Finally, as Hodson (2005) has demonstrated, codification of duties and responsibilities in an operating agreement, clear policies addressing use of foundation funds and development expenses, and candid reciprocal communication can mitigate the potential for conflict stemming from an individual's dual role as foundation chief executive and institutional advancement officer.

Foundation Independence

The growth of foundation resources, expansion of the scope of foundation activities, and concerns about control and oversight of foundation resources have led some institutional presidents and boards to attempt to exercise more direct control over affiliated foundations. Conversely, foundation staff and boards may believe that a significant degree of autonomy is essential to their ability to fulfill their role as fiduciaries, stewards, and fundraisers. Discussions about foundation-institution relationships have, accordingly, often focused on the appropriate degree of foundation independence. In an influential white paper titled "State University-Related Foundations and the Issue of Independence," Roha outlined seven "touchstones of foundation independence" (2000). Roha's analysis was based on two fundamental assumptions. First, foundations have an obligation to safeguard the privacy of donor records and have a strong interest in safeguarding "trade secrets" concerning donor prospects, business decisions, development strategies, and investment strategies. Second, extension of state freedom-of-information laws to foundations would compromise the privacy of foundation records, practices, and strategies; undermine foundations' capacity to effectively raise and manage private resources; and impose undue compliance burdens. Roha found that courts typically decided whether state freedom-of-information laws applicable to government entities also covered affiliated foundations by testing the degree to which foundations were "independent" of their affiliated institution. "Independence," in turn, was determined by a facts-and-circumstances test that looked at the degree of institutional control of the foundation board, whether the foundation paid its own staff, its use of university office space, and the like. Many foundation executives and boards took Roha's analysis to heart, striving to establish their legal independence as a means of reinforcing the corporate veil separating the state institution and the foundation, as well as safeguarding the privacy of their donors and business information.

Although foundation independence has been seen as a means of safeguarding donors' privacy and avoiding burdensome restrictions applicable to state entities, independence *is* also frequently associated with organizational maturity. *College and University Foundations: Serving America's Public Higher Education* outlined two classification systems, both of which associated foundation autonomy with active leadership and control of fundraising, expanded roles for foundation board members and staff, and organizational maturity and sophistication (Hedgepeth, 1997). The association among independence, fundraising capacity, and organizational sophistication derives from several factors. For example, budgetary independence allows foundations to make sustained strategic investments in development programs and operations that might not be possible for foundations relying on financial support from the institution. Independence may also enhance foundations' ability to attract influential and highly engaged board members and offer a competitive advantage in staff recruitment and retention. An independent foundation may be better able to focus on long-term investment objectives, build operating reserves, manage liquidity and debt, and sustain other forward-looking financial strategies in the face of inevitable and sometimes short-sighted pressures for current spending. Finally, and most important, a degree of independence may be essential to foundations' ability to serve as effective stewards of privately contributed assets. An independent foundation can serve a watchdog function, monitoring how donor-restricted funds are used and even shielding institution staff from pressure to use privately contributed funds inappropriately or imprudently.

In recent years, changes in the legal and political landscapes have influenced how foundation and institution leaders think about foundations' independence. In 2005, the Iowa Supreme Court ruled that the state's freedom-of-information laws applied to the Iowa State University Foundation, even though it demonstrated a high degree of independence. The court opined that the foundation was performing a core function of a government entity in its capacity as the primary fundraiser for the university, and that a government entity could not skirt freedom-of-information laws by contracting core functions to private (nongovernment) entities. Although the ruling derived from the specifics of Iowa law and applied only to universities in that state, it confirmed a growing consensus that institutionally related foundations, regardless of their degree of legal independence, should conform to the highest standards of transparency compatible with the safeguarding of donor privacy.

The Iowa ruling was in keeping with federal calls for heightened accountability for charities. As chair and later as ranking member of the Senate Finance Committee, Senator Charles Grassley staged a high-profile series of hearings focused on abuses of the charitable tax deduction and other potential abuses of exempt status by donors and charities. In the fall of 2007 the committee conducted hearings questioning the endowment spending practices of colleges and universities and the tax exemptions associated with offshore investments held by charities. Following Grassley's lead, the Internal Revenue Service has undertaken a comprehensive compliance review of endowments, unrelated business taxable income, and executive compensation at colleges and universities. Common to all of these examinations was the assumption that charities must be held to a high standard of transparency to ensure that they are not being used to skirt taxes or exploit personal benefit, but to ensure they are providing societal benefits commensurate with their financial resources. Such a political climate renders the invocation of "privacy" decidedly problematic as a rationale for independence. As suggested earlier, however, institutional control of foundations could significantly undermine their capacity to serve as fundraisers, stewards of private resources, and vehicles for engaging volunteer leadership of the highest caliber.

Conclusion

As public institutions' development programs evolve and mature, it seems likely presidents and boards will need to shift their focus away from the goals of institutional control or foundation independence, and toward exploring how foundations and institutions can most effectively work together to advance both institutional priorities and the philanthropic interests of their donors. For some institutions and foundations, this might entail enhancing financial practices and controls, developing more sophisticated systems to ensure compliance with donor intent and accountability concerning endowment spending, and restructuring fundraising operations. It will also require (1) strategically cultivating volunteer leadership in much the same way that institutions cultivate relationships with prospective donors; (2) identifying the core capacities and attributes necessary to support the evolving mission of foundations; (3) engaging alumni, community leaders, and other institutional constituents in a variety of advisory and volunteer roles; and (4) grooming the best prospects for leadership as foundation board members. Finally, institution and foundation boards will need to work closely to clarify their respective roles; support development functions throughout the institution; and maintain candor, collaboration, and the capacity to constructively manage the inevitable conflicts.

References

Association of Governing Boards of Universities and Colleges. "Illustrative Memorandum of Understanding Between a Foundation and Host Institution or System," 2005. Retrieved Nov. 30, 2009, from http://www.case.org/Browse_by_Professional_Interest/Institutionally_Related_Foundations/AGB-CASE_Memorandum_of_Understanding.html.

Bass, D., and Lanier, J. "What Lies Ahead for University-Foundation Relations?" *Trusteeship*, 2008, 16(6), 15–19.

Colorado State Auditor. *University of Colorado Foundation Performance Audit*. Report control no. 1691, 2005.

Council for Aid to Education (1978–2008), n.d. Voluntary Support of Education. Retrieved from http://www.cae.org/content/pro_data_trends.htm.

Grant Thornton LLP. "Kansas Board of Regents Confidential Exit Analysis Related to the Retirement of Dr. Jon Wefald, President of Kansas State University." 2009. Kansas Board of Regents, Topeka, KS.

Hedgepeth, R. C. "Creating a Successful Institutionally Related Foundation." In J. F. Phelan (ed.), *College and University Foundations: Serving America's Public Higher Education.* Washington, D.C.: Association of Governing Boards of Universities and Colleges, 1997.

Hodson, J. B. *The Dual Role of Public University Administrator and Executive of an Institutionally-Related Foundation: A Multiple Case Study.* Unpublished doctoral dissertation, Department of Educational Administration, University of Nebraska, Lincoln, 2005.

Kaplan, A. E. *2008 Voluntary Support of Education.* New York: Council for Aid to Education, 2009.

KU Endowment Association. "Frequently Asked Questions" (n.d.). Retrieved Nov. 17, 2009, from http://www.kuendowment.org/faqs/.

Legon, R. D. (ed.). *Margin of Excellence: The New Work of Higher Education Foundations.* Washington, D.C.: Association of Governing Boards of Universities and Colleges, 2005.

Pocock, J. W. *Fundraising Leadership: A Guide for College and University Boards.* Washington, D.C.: Association of Governing Boards of Universities and Colleges, 1989.

Roha, T. A. "State University-Related Foundations and the Issue of Independence." *AGB Occasional Paper no. 39.* Washington, D.C.: Association of Governing Boards of Universities and Colleges, 2000.

Schrum, J. B. *A Board's Guide to Comprehensive Campaigns.* Washington, D.C.: Association of Governing Boards of Universities and Colleges, 2000.

Schwartz, M., and Akins, L. *Policies, Practices, and Composition of Governing Boards of Public Colleges and Universities.* Washington, D.C.: Association of Governing Boards of Universities and Colleges, 2004.

DAVID BASS is the director of foundation programs for the Association of Governing Boards of Universities and Colleges in Washington, D.C.

3

Universities use various mechanisms to fund the development operation, including gift taxes, management fees, unrestricted giving, and earnings on cash holdings. Much in the way of planning how best to fund fundraising is required before you hire a single major gift officer or start an annual giving program.

The Challenge of Funding Fundraising

Robert J. Holmes, Jr.

Public higher education has grown to appreciate added support from charitable gifts. In fact public institutions, like private institutions, have become reliant on philanthropic resources for building facilities, supplementing current operations, and supplying revenue from endowments for operations. The need for charitable gifts is not new. Philanthropic support for public higher education reaches back to the early 1900s, when public universities needed funding assistance to build campus facilities because state funds were stretched thin. To facilitate the process of acquiring, receiving, and processing gifts, and managing and investing those charitable resources, universities established institutionally related foundations (IRFs). Some foundations were created with a role of directing a formal fundraising program, while others placed their focus on funds management. Regardless of the role for the foundations, universities have grown to rely on charitable gifts for annual operational supplements, capital purposes, or endowed funds. Building endowments to deliver a recurring source of support in perpetuity became an attractive resource as state budgets were strained for other broadening social priorities. One could view charitable resources as the third leg of the stool for funding a public institution, along with tuition and fees as well as grants. To be certain, these are unequal legs, but they have emerged as essential sources.

The inequality of the legs has changed over time as state appropriations for higher education decreased. Public universities were described in the 1960s and earlier as "state-supported." Tuition was set low intentionally to allow access to higher education for the broader community. However, as educational costs rose and states balanced competing demands on tax sources, tuition as a source grew rapidly in many states, especially in New England.

NEW DIRECTIONS FOR HIGHER EDUCATION, no. 149, Spring 2010 © Wiley Periodicals, Inc.
Published online in Wiley InterScience (www.interscience.wiley.com) • DOI: 10.1002/he.378

To preserve the commitment of access for all those with the ability to tackle a higher education curriculum, charitable gifts for scholarships grew as an institutional priority. Universities began to reach for supplemental funding in retaining and attracting faculty, creating opportunities for donors to answer the call to recruit a new faculty member by combining philanthropy with state funding.

Both need-based and merit-based scholarships merged as a high priority for universities as they worked to accomplish their mission of delivering high-quality education with access to all who qualified academically. Competition among institutions to attract particularly talented faculty presented a mushrooming demand for resources beyond what states could appropriate.

As the public's expectations grew for high-quality, affordable education, there was pressure to look more to philanthropy as an additional resource. At the same time state budgets were feeling pressure to respond to social issues other than appropriations for education, universities turned to tuition increases as a solution. Thus began the shifting of the responsibility for financing high-quality, affordable education from solely state appropriations and tuition to state appropriations, tuition, grants and contracts, and philanthropy. Granted they remain even today unequal legs to the funding stool; however, they do represent the essential resources required to deliver the quality education the public has grown to expect. The quality of the education would be significantly limited without the philanthropy component. The more mature the institution or its foundation has become, the more reliant—even dependent—the institution is on charitable support.

From Start-up Foundation to Mature Foundation

Responding to the expectations of communities to have this high-quality university experience, institutions have turned to formal development of fundraising efforts. For private institutions, this is nothing new, but for public universities the emergence of philanthropy grew exponentially in the twentieth century, with no end currently in sight. Therefore, creating IRFs to facilitate this task became a high priority. The Council for Advancement and Support of Education (CASE) has catalogued articles that describe the rationale and the benefits of using an IRF. In most instances, foundations can perform many functions without the requirements and restrictions placed on their parent institution by the state. Whether the task is receiving, processing, managing, or investing charitable gifts, foundations within their IRS charter as a 501(c)(3) organization can facilitate the process more advantageously than their institution. The other element that has significant attractiveness for donors is the ability of most foundations to maintain confidentiality of donors' gifts and the details surrounding those gifts. The board of the foundation plays an integral role as a fiduciary for those donors whose gifts were placed in their trust.

Whether the institution is young or old, or whether its IRF is a start-up, emerging, or mature organization, the challenges of responding to the escalating financial demands of the parent university persist and are stronger than ever. IRFs have frequently been described as dependent, interdependent, or independent in their relationship. It is important to examine the relationship of the IRF to its parent university. How the IRF relates to its parent university depends on its operational funding or funding model. Whether an IRF is start-up, emerging, or mature, of course, relates to its age and fundraising success. The dependence status may be philosophical. However, the CASE 2006 Survey of IRFs showed that a high percentage of IRFs are either interdependent or independent. These foundations also actively pursue and carry the charge of serving the institution as its primary fundraising organization. Some public institutions have more than one IRF, and those foundations are likely to be specific to an academic discipline.

Funding Fundraising

With a greater supply of potential donors and an unending thirst by the university for charitable resources, the only element holding up success in securing charitable support is funding the cost of fundraising. Unfortunately, success in fundraising does not come immediately with the investment of added operational resources. Making an immediate investment for the purpose of generating gifts even with a compelling story does not create an immediate flow of resources. It is not like turning on the faucet and having gift funding flow to the institution. Relationships with prospective donors must come first and most often take time.

As seasoned professionals responsible for building philanthropy programs know so well, the return on the investment can take months or years. However, if the investment is delayed or does not use every source available, the return will be less than the potential and slower to materialize than expected or required. To make money requires an investment, and the return on investment can in turn support the institutionally related foundation, as the funding scenarios presented here demonstrate.

Institutional Support. The institution in many cases furnishes funding at some level to the IRF. The CASE 2006 Survey found that 35 percent of those responding to its survey used institutional funding, and that it represented 39 percent of the budget. The 2009 Survey by CASE found that the percentage of budget remained the same, but the number of IRFs using institutional support increased from 35 to 52 percent.

As gifts begin to accumulate, the other operating sources that relate to gifts can allow reduction in reliance on institutional support or the ability to reduce fees. Because of the economic climate, FY2010 IRFs show an increase in use of this source. Fees on gifts and fees from the endowment can lessen the requirement for institutional funds.

How much in institutional (or state) resources should be committed to this investment can become a debated topic. If the state shrinks its appropriation to the institution, or if the institution's growth of enrolled students outstrips the state's funding to the institution to deliver the education, the rationale to increase institutional funding to the IRF becomes a difficult sell. To add to the debate, the institution's support to the IRF generates a return on investment of charitable gifts that is most often restricted by the donor. To add further to the debate, gifts for endowed purposes return only 3.5–5 percent to the institution depending on the IRF's investment policy on spending. On the opposing side of the debate, if potential charitable sources for institutions exist among its constituencies and the donor community responds to institutional priorities, it should be deemed a wise investment for the university to keep funding the IRF at some level.

Unrestricted Gifts. With so many specific and compelling needs across the institution to be met through annual support from donors, attracting unrestricted gifts becomes a significant challenge. In fact, the CASE 2006 Survey shows widespread use of this source, with 78 percent of respondents applying unrestricted funds, but those funds accounted for only 10 percent of the operating budgets. In addition, some IRFs have endowment funds created to supply unrestricted funds for operational purposes, but those endowed gifts remain limited in number in most cases.

Management Fees from the Endowment. The IRF's investment committee usually determines a management fee in consultation with the IRF's finance committee. Policies for the IRF should state how the fee is determined and when it is applied. Policies often indicate that the fee will be revisited annually. This fee can generate revenue that can become the mainstay of funding for the IRF. For mature foundations with large endowments, the funds generated from the fee can be sizable, and most important it furnishes recurring revenue for operations more consistently and reliably than most sources do.

The fees may range from 1 to 4 percent of the fair market value of the endowment portfolio. The size of the fee affects the investment total return target and risk profile. The CASE 2006 Survey showed 68 percent of foundations using this source, and those funds represented 39 percent of the IRF operating budget. The number of foundations using this source has increased to 80 percent, as noted by the CASE 2009 Survey, but the impact on the budget remains at 39 percent.

Gifts Fee. Many foundations administer a one-time fee on gifts. Some charge this fee only on nonendowed gifts; others apply the fee across the board. They may begin small with a 1 percent fee, but with pressure to increase operational revenues for further investment in fundraising or as a result of difficult economic conditions as witnessed in the recent economic downturn, it can increase to 5 percent or higher.

Temporary Investment Earnings. Another significant source for funding the IRF comes from income and appreciation of the gifts that are nonendowed as well as those awaiting placement in the endowment fund. From the CASE 2006 Survey, 78 percent of foundations use this source, and it represented 21 percent of the foundation's operating budget. The CASE 2009 Survey reflects an increase in use of this source to 86 percent of those responding. Most IRF investment policies give guidance to the manner of investment of these funds to maximize the return while weighing the associated risk and preservation of principal, since these funds could be called on by the host institution at any time. However, these funds may also be placed in investment categories according to the timing of their eventual use. Gifts for annual support may be for immediate use and require greater investment liquidity. Gifts for building projects might be accumulated for a few years, allowing investment strategies that would deliver a higher return.

Revenues from Real Estate. Some foundations own income-producing real estate properties. These properties likely bear a direct relationship to fulfilling needs of the institution and must pertain to the nonprofit mission of the foundation. Ownership of properties, such as office buildings for faculty, research facilities, classroom buildings, or student housing purchased by the IRF to benefit the parent institution, may generate positive revenues but must be coupled with a strong commitment by the institution to be a tenant. The CASE 2006 Survey reflected 19 percent of IRFs using this resource while representing an average of 15 percent of the operating budget. Those foundations using real estate have increased to 27 percent, judging from the CASE 2009 Survey. The median for operating budgets in the survey results was 7 percent. The figure was skewed as a result of two foundations that indicated their real estate revenues furnished in excess of 60 percent for operations. Some real estate properties owned by the IRF could also have mixed use to include retail or commercial tenants. The IRF must remain clear on its appetite for risk when owning real estate and must maintain a prudent reserve to cover downturns or natural disasters.

Other Sources. Building the right funding model for the IRF depends on decisions related to dependence on the host university and the philosophical positioning of the role of the IRF to serve as an active fundraising arm of the institution. Those decisions will drive the policy for selection and integration of all available revenue sources.

Several other sources can help support the IRF, depending on its responsibilities. For example, if the institution's alumni magazine falls under the expenses of the IRF, opportunities may exist for advertising revenue. Also, alumni associations commonly secure revenues from affiliation agreements. These associations may fall under the umbrella of the IRF, or they may be separately incorporated as an IRC 501(c)(3) organization and fully use those agreements for their own operating budgets. The pros and cons of the sources I have discussed are listed here.

Institutional Support
Pros

- A clearly defined statement of value gets delivered when the institution invests in the IRF.
- The university's investment also helps to ensure that the IRF remains in a tight orbit around its parent institution.
- University funding of the IRF shows a commitment to the philanthropic charge and mission of the IRF.
- A healthy interdependency occurs with a funding partnership.
- Since the IRF was created only for the purpose of serving its parent institution, joint funding keeps the priorities of the IRF aligned with the institution's priorities.
- The institution's support lessens the pressure on high gift-related fees, and this in turn makes more of the donor's gift available for its intended purpose.
- University funding is generally a reliable and recurring source. Only in a significant economic downturn would this source be threatened with reduction or elimination. The latest recession has reduced university support for many IRFs.

Cons

- Though a positive of the institution's contribution to the operating budget of the IRF is its recurring nature, it is subject to reduction when the institution is under financial pressure in state budget challenges.
- Competing for institutional funds with academic programs could create a public relations issue on campus. This can become even more stressful if unrestricted state funds are spent to raise charitable funds that are returned as restricted purpose gifts.
- Funding from the institution at the college unit budget level can create a debate about the best use of the development officer's time. A clear and concise position description can head off the tendency for the college-funded employee to stray from the focus on philanthropy.
- Although some problems can occur with overweighting university support of an IRF related to its separate IRS status, creating an agreement between the institution and the foundation that articulates the role, mission, and purpose of the foundation should handle any misunderstandings.

Unrestricted Gifts
Pros

- Unrestricted gifts permit ample flexibility for the foundation in funding the operating budget.

NEW DIRECTIONS FOR HIGHER EDUCATION • DOI: 10.1002/he

- Unrestricted gifts free the organization from critical review by the academic community.
- Using unrestricted gifts adds another source to the funding model, which helps to maximize every available source for the investment in gift generation.

Cons

- The amount of revenue generated by these gifts may be difficult to predict, which can create budget issues. It may or may not be a recurring source.
- The unrestricted gifts often come from many smaller gifts. This could create a difficult donor relations response to those who might believe their gifts are less important than larger ones that go to academic priorities.
- If all unrestricted giving is directed to operations, the "case" for renewal is weakened. Eventually, the donors will aim their giving at some restricted purpose that has more meaning to them and more direct impact on students and faculty.
- An analysis of the cost per dollar raised for unrestricted gifts may reflect a less-than-positive picture.
- The source of funds presents a difficult challenge for staff in presenting the need. As a donor, funding operations has a weak appeal.

Management Fee on Endowments
Pros

- The fee generates a recurring source of revenue and, in most economic climates, serves as a reliable source.
- With the success of fundraising for endowed purposes, the fee will generate an increasing amount each year, especially in an appreciating investment climate.
- This fee seems to be considered by donors to be an accounting matter and one less irritating than investment fees, which are considered normal.

Cons

- The fee adds a challenge to the investment committee to recommend policies that deliver sufficient total return to cover a spending level that is acceptable to university leaders and donors, all the while leaving funds available to adjust for inflation. Keeping the fee as low as possible enables a reasonable spending percentage to the campus beneficiaries but still provides the valuable recurring operating revenue so essential for organizational stability.
- Some policies for the IRF may curtail charging the fee when the fair market value of the portfolio drops below the "historic" or gift value.

- The amount of revenue from this fee is essentially a function of the endowment size and the percentage fee, per the policy.

Gift Fees
Pros

- Fees assessed on gifts received can generate a solid and primary source of revenue.
- As long as the fees are properly acknowledged to donors, in most situations the fee is recognized as an administrative cost of doing the business of fundraising.
- In most economic climates, the fee revenue can be reasonably forecast in advance of the budget year.
- The fees are spread across the entire donor population. In mature foundations that receive lump sum gifts of $1 million or more, it is not uncommon to decrease the fee gradually as the size of the gift increases. Stepping down the fee at the higher multimillion-dollar gift level sits better with both the donor and the institutional beneficiary.

Cons

- Some donors will object to the fee. An important step in dealing with the objections would be to outline in writing a foundation policy for these situations. If this fee serves as an integral part of the funding model, expenses are no doubt budgeted against that revenue. So the IRF can create a written resolution to handle such objections, such as having the foundation executive committee authorize waiver of the fee in special circumstances.
- Fees on capital projects must be accounted for in the budget for a building. Projects usually include fees from architects, engineers, and consultants, so a fee on gifts to support the fundraising project should be no different than what it is for other fundraising projects.
- Institutional beneficiaries of the gifts can complain about the fees and make objections. In fact, they could even advise donors how to sidestep the foundation by processing gifts through another organization on campus that does not administer a fee. A firm institutional policy guiding gifts can avert an end run. This breakdown can cause other dominolike reactions to occur, such as losing accurate historical records of donor gifts.
- A solution to the objections of administering a fee on capital gifts may be to cover the fee amount from the academic unit's annual fund. Even an appeal to the institution's central administration might furnish the foundation with funds represented by the fee. Some institutional foundations permit temporary investment earnings to generate fee equivalency. However, if temporary investment earnings are already part of the model, then there would be no gain from that action.

Nonendowed Gift Earnings
Pros

- This revenue stream can also be substantial and reasonably predictable on the basis of the historic levels of account balances and inbound flow of gifts that are spendable.
- This source would represent an accounting transaction and be less onerous to donors since it preserves the entirety of the gift.

Cons

- The gifts must have a certain degree of liquidity, so measures must be taken to carefully estimate the average daily balance since they are spendable funds and could be called on by the institution over the course of the year.
- Some thrifty and sophisticated donors of capital projects may object to the earnings going to a general fundraising purpose and not to the building associated with their gift. Explaining the foundation funding model to the donors will help.
- The investment policy must outline a clear statement noting the need for preservation of principal.

Real Estate Revenues
Pros

- If the revenue comes from office space in buildings owned by the foundation with a mix of for-profit and university use, the source can be quite reliable.
- If the revenue comes from student housing where the land or improvements are owned by the foundation, the source can be as reliable as fluctuation of enrollment and the competition in the marketplace.
- The flow of revenue to the foundation can be reasonably predictable.
- This strategy of real estate ownership assists the institution with acquiring select properties while generating revenue to invest in fundraising, lessening reliance on university funding or fees on gifts.
- Other related and creative business options can add revenue to the operations budget, such as rental of parking areas owned by the IRF.

Cons

Depending on the real estate source, reliability as recurring revenue has some risk:

- In the commercial office space example, an economic downturn would lower the for-profit occupancy rate owing to inability to maintain the lease.
- With the student housing example, any loss of rentable space to students that is due to a hurricane or fire would be detrimental to net income.

• Management of the real estate portfolio brings a cost, so care must be taken to factor in all expenses of facilities management, strategic oversight, and financial management of the active real estate portfolio.

Other Revenues

• Some foundations will successfully use special events for generating operating revenue. Although these events yield several benefits even beyond additional operating revenues, they generally are staff- and volunteer-intensive.
• Patents and copyrights have been noted as additional sources in special circumstances. There may be a lag time in generation of income, and the source may be for restricted purposes.

The Funding Model

When an institution and its IRF analyze the means needed to expand its foundation's operating budget, consideration must be given to the philosophical direction. Should the foundation become a dependent, interdependent, or independent foundation? Since most institutions have an insatiable thirst for charitable support to fulfill their mission, and since most institutions have an ample supply of prospects, the conclusion drawn may be to take every means possible to generate operating revenue. The range of these fees can be retrieved from such sources as annual surveys by the National Association of College and University Business Officers (NACUBO) or the College and University Professional Association (CUPA). The population of other IRFs has created a pool of data with respected tolerance for gift-related fees. The opportunities for real estate revenue will be a function of the geographic location of the institution and the IRF with its special circumstances. That leaves the institutional investment. The mix of these sources defined by policies creates the funding model for an institution. The model pictured in Table 3.1 is an example of an IRF budget.

If a foundation's current budget lacks any of these sources, then close examination of the return on investment of the invested operational funds may assist in inclusion of, or increase in, revenue sources.

When Is Investment of Operating Revenues Enough?

If the national mission of public higher education focuses on greater access to higher education and at that same time is devoted to improved quality of that education, then funding from state, tuition, federal grants, and the current level of philanthropy will continue to be insufficient. So the pressure on any one of these sources will only grow in the years to come as the federal government and the states wrestle with demand for social services and families seek solutions to rising tuition. The role of philanthropy as an

Table 3.1 A Funding Model

Source	Percentage of Operating Budget		
	Original FY09	Revised FY09*	FY10 Projected
University central funding	23%	24%	23%
University unit funding	6%	6%	7%
Endowment fees (currently at 2%)	21%	19%	20%
Gift fee on inbound gifts (at 3%)	8%	8%	8%
Unrestricted gifts	2%	1%	1%
Nonendowed gift earnings	9%	1%	8%
Carry forward and reserves	8%	17%	5%
Endowment for operations spendable	>1%	>1%	>1%
Real estate: off-campus student housing	8%	10%	12%
Real estate and management fees: office buildings rental revenue	14%	14%	15%

Note: *Revised to the economic downturn of 2008 and 2009.

ingredient in funding higher education remains an essential part of fulfilling the mission of access and quality in public higher education. The need for more charitable support is sure to grow. So when is the operating revenue for an IRF enough? Never.

ROBERT J. HOLMES, JR., is the vice president for alumni relations and development at the University of Central Florida. He also serves as the CEO of the University of Central Florida Foundation.

NEW DIRECTIONS FOR HIGHER EDUCATION • DOI: 10.1002/he

4

Although professional staff can assist with parts of the fundraising enterprise, presidents and deans play the leading role in cultivating and soliciting major gifts to benefit the academic enterprise.

Leading the Way: The Role of Presidents and Academic Deans in Fundraising

J. Bradford Hodson

University presidents and academic deans lead; it's what the institution and its many constituents expect of them. Presidents lead institutions through the mundane and the revolutionary. They inspire a shared vision and illuminate the path that leads to realization of that vision. Academic deans lead faculty and programs. They facilitate faculty achievement in student learning, discovery, and engagement. The concept of actively leading constituents, internal and external, is second nature to many university administrators in most areas, except one: fundraising.

For many university presidents and academic deans, it's a part of the job that is not well defined or well understood. They know there is an expectation that private funds will flow into the university or its academic colleges, but their specific role remains a mystery. This uncertainty may be due to fundraising recently becoming an expectation of leadership, particularly at public institutions; lack of experience on the part of presidents and deans in soliciting private gifts; or the belief of institutional leaders that such activities are beneath them. In frustration or desperation, they abdicate their leadership of fundraising to a development staff who then pick up the pieces and carry on as best they can.

In reality, fundraising is a shared responsibility among a wide group of institutional leaders (Glier, 2004), most notably the university's president and the deans of its academic colleges. Individuals in these positions play a key role in creating and sustaining a vibrant culture of philanthropy and private

New Directions for Higher Education, no. 149, Spring 2010 © Wiley Periodicals, Inc.
Published online in Wiley InterScience (www.interscience.wiley.com) • DOI: 10.1002/he.379

39

support. Leadership in the area of fundraising is quickly becoming an expectation rather than an extracurricular activity. As Kaufman (2004) noted, "Fundraising is one of the most visible and demanding roles expected from campus leaders today" (p. 50). Given the increasing frequency with which fundraising is viewed as a measure of the effectiveness of presidents and academic deans, a clear understanding of the expectations for both positions is essential.

The President: Fundraiser-in-Chief

As with nearly all institutional activities, the university president shoulders the ultimate responsibility for the success of the fundraising program. So much of what precedes effective cultivation and solicitation of major gifts must come from the president. No other institutional officer can create the vision, establish university-wide priorities, or make the case for support as effectively as the president. All are important elements of successful fundraising. Because of the key visioning and priority-setting roles the president plays, "the ultimate responsibility for fundraising cannot be delegated to the staff, the [governing] board, or the foundation board" (Fisher, 1985, p. 51). Whereas in the past university presidents saw their role in fundraising as limited to hiring a staff of professionals to raise private gifts, presidents today are beginning to view their personal involvement as being critical to augmenting the work of the professional fundraising staff (Miller, 1991).

Because his or her personal involvement is so important, the university president should give fundraising the same status and priority as other parts of the job. Rather than being viewed as an isolated or "special" activity, fundraising should be viewed by the president as part of his or her role of securing financing for the institution (Slinker, 1988). Just as the president of a public institution engages the legislature to secure additional appropriations, activities such as cultivating and soliciting donors are also part of the president's role of obtaining funds to ensure the short-term survival and long-term growth of the institution.

Creating a Compelling Vision. First and foremost among the president's fundraising responsibilities is creation and communication of a vision for the institution that excites and inspires constituents to provide financial support. As Fisher (1985, p. 51) said, "It always comes back to the president. The president is the person with the vision, who inspires donor confidence, who creates the climate in which the fundraising activities take place."

Fisher (1985, p. 50) goes on to note, "The president personifies the institution." The president's vision for the university becomes a shared vision in the hearts and minds of constituents. For fundraising to be successful, constituents must adopt the president's vision for the university and take some level of responsibility for realization of that vision (Fisher, 1985).

Setting Institutional Priorities. The university president is also responsible for leading the institution-wide discussion that takes his or her vision and breaks it down into actionable, strategic priorities. From these priorities, fundraising goals will be developed that can be understood and supported by all levels of the institution. Because competition for resources within the university can be acute, the president becomes responsible for determining the institution's most significant financial needs for which private gifts will be sought (Essex and Ansbach, 1993). This process is usually closely aligned with the strategic planning process of the institution. Willmer (1993, p. 37), however, cautions that the list of university needs and priorities "should not exceed the realistic expectations of what can be funded through institutional advancement. The president should temper his or her ideas and goals to match the overall [fundraising] potential of the university."

Articulating the Case for Support. As the primary spokesperson for the institution, the university president is expected to articulate how donors' charitable gifts will enhance the academy. Major donors in particular like to feel as if they are being involved in something strategic and well thought out. They want to know about the president's vision and the institution's strategic direction, along with the resources the university needs to get there. Conversations between the president and prospective major donors should also focus on what the donor wants his or her gift to accomplish. In the end, the case for support—why the donor should make a major gift to support a pre-identified institutional need—should be centered on the donor's aspirations for the gift. Weidner (2008, p. 397) notes the "wonderfully conspiratorial nature of major gift fundraising." According to him, "It is fun to listen to the donor and use what they say to craft a gift that is meaningful to the donor and to the school. It is important to listen to the donors rather than drive hard with your own notion of an end result."

Assessing Institutional Readiness. Only the president can determine if the university is prepared to launch a fundraising initiative. Readiness for fundraising includes not only such factors as having a clear vision for the university and strategic priorities that will resonate with prospective donors and afford sufficient fundraising potential, but also possessing a professional staff with the expertise and budget to get the job done (Kaufman, 2004), and a commitment from the president of their time and energy to lead the campaign to successful completion. Seeking external fundraising counsel is often very useful, particularly if the president is unsure of how to judge readiness or if the president knows a great deal of change needs to take place before a fundraising campaign can be launched. Counsel can be of particular use on the latter when changes in staff, an increase in operating budgets, or expanded commitments from advisory groups such as the foundation board will be required. This type of information is often better accepted from a third-party "expert" than from internal staff or the president.

Empowering Constituents. As the university's most visible leader, it falls to the president to inspire and empower internal and external constituents to join in the fundraising enterprise.

Inspiring Donor Confidence. Donors give to organizations that they trust will use their charitable gifts in a way that conforms to their wishes. Such trust is most often based on relationships formed between the leaders of the organization and the donors. Because strong relationships follow from repeated interaction, Satterwhite (2004, p. 51) notes that the president's involvement in fundraising "is not limited to a minimal number of appearances, speeches, or hosted functions." He says, "The president must maintain a level of availability to prospective donors. Donors have a stronger sense of dedication to a campaign if they see a heavy presidential involvement and have significant access to the president."

Invest in External Relationships. The president must be a visible, accessible leader. Prospective donors at all giving levels must come to know the president as an engaged and vibrant leader of the university and of the community. According to Kaufman (2004), "A president who is distracted by his or her love of an academic discipline or who remains in a comfort zone that is exclusively associated with the internal [university] community is not likely to be a successful fundraiser" (p. 50). The president should rarely miss an opportunity to engage external constituents. Although some constituents may themselves lack interest in the university's programs or the financial capacity to make a charitable gift, their word-of-mouth endorsement of the president's leadership to those constituents who do have interest and capacity is invaluable.

Encouraging Faculty and Staff Participation. Presidents desirous of engaging constituents should not overlook faculty and staff. It is unrealistic to believe that all faculty and staff will become actively engaged in fundraising, but their support of the president's work in this area is helpful. Also, Weidner (2008, p. 394) noted that "alumni tend to give because of their gratitude for the way they were treated by individual faculty members." Getting faculty involved in cultivation and solicitation of alumni and friends who admire their work or their commitment to the institution will enhance the likelihood that a request for financial support will be accepted.

Cultivating and Soliciting Gifts. Individuals who themselves have great wealth or who manage wealth on behalf of a corporation or foundation often respond best when talking to the man or woman in charge—the president. Professional fundraising staff should be respectful of the president's time commitment to fundraising and only include him in the conversation if his presence will add value. The president should remember that there are times when the only reason that he is in the room is because he is the living embodiment of the university. Presidents who become comfortable with this fact are able to state the case for private support with passion and ease.

The president should also recognize that the long-term nature of donor relationships is that they exist between the donor and the university, not with the president personally. The president, academic deans, faculty members, and professional fundraising staff are merely agents acting on behalf of the university (Kvet and Stewart, 2009). Eckert and Pollack (2000) cautioned that while your request for support may, in your mind, be the culmination of the relationship with a prospect, in fact, to the prospect, it is but one moment in their long relationship with the university.

Thanking and Recognizing Donors. Just as a charitable solicitation from the president carries special meaning, so too does a thank-you from the president. Gifts of a certain level should be recognized with a note from the president, or in the case of a major gift a phone call. Both types of recognition are a function of the president's time commitment to fundraising and the ability of staff to make the calls and letters happen in a timely manner. All donor recognition should focus on helping the donors see the good their gifts have done for the students and the university (Kvet and Stewart, 2009). It's always effective to use real examples of how a particular gift made something larger or special happen for the university or a particular student.

Also, as presidents thank and recognize donors, they should keep in mind that many donors view their gift not as a donation but as an investment in the institution. "Donors are looking for results," said Eckert and Pollack (2000, p. 47). "Individuals want to know exactly how many students benefited from their gifts. This desire for greater accountability is a result of decreased public confidence in educational institutions, especially government- funded ones."

The Academic Dean: An Evolving Role in Fundraising

Much of what has been said here about the role of the president in leading the fundraising effort can be applied to academic deans on the smaller scale of an academic school or college. Although deans serve both academic and administrative roles, the traditional responsibility of a dean is to ensure the quality of the programs in her school or college, something of great interest to donors. This focus on program quality has evolved over time from being "almost exclusively student focused to include a multi-faceted array of roles, such as budgeting and fundraising, personnel and work environment management, program oversight, and external public relations" (Wolverton, Gmelch, Montez, and Nies, 2001, p. 6). This change in focus has come as a result of a change in how higher education is funded. As colleges and universities deal with rising costs, decreasing state support, and limits on tuition increases, academic deans see added pressure to become advocates for external funds from private donors, to keep technology up-to-date, finance research, and recruit and retain bright new faculty members (Sheehan and Mihailidis, 2007).

Setting Academic Priorities. Just as the university president determines what the university's fundraising priorities will be, the dean performs the same task for the academic college. It goes without saying that the priorities identified by the academic dean at the school or college level should feed into the larger institutional strategic and fundraising plans. Academic deans should keep in mind that donors respond to fundraising priories that are actionable and result in quantifiable results. Lofty dreams that seem unattainable or that have negligible effects on programs or students do not resonate with major donors.

Facilitating Faculty Partnerships. Faculty often expect to have the dean's full attention on faculty, curricular, and student affairs. A dean who appears to be focused too much on fundraising or external relations risks losing the internal support of the faculty. There is, however, a balance that can be struck. Weidner (2008, p. 394) advises that "the more [a dean] becomes a successful fundraiser or otherwise an 'outside' dean, the more important it is for the faculty to see [that person] approach [his or her] job with humility and with a sense of [the faculty's] importance."

Faculty can be enormously helpful in fundraising. The dean should engage faculty as partners in fundraising, asking them to join in on donor visits and collaborate with the dean on crafting the case for support. As was stated earlier, alumni often give because they were treated well by a particular faculty member. In this regard, faculty are as critical to the success of fundraising as they are to the success of the college's academic programs (Weidner, 2008).

Identify Prospects. Because academic deans operate closer to the front lines—closer to students—than university presidents, they are in a far better position to identify prospective donors, particularly from the ranks of alumni. Deans should begin by thinking about former students who now have executive jobs in industry. The dean can also identify other prospective donors, such as industry leaders who are not alumni and corporations that have an interest in hiring graduates or benefiting from research. Faculty can also be helpful in this process. The dean should communicate the name of a prospective donor to the professional fundraising staff, who can then advise the dean of that person's giving history and how best to approach the prospect to ask for a gift. Eckert and Pollack (2000) reminded academic deans and faculty that "sharing [prospect] information is not giving away 'your' donors. Rather it will ensure that one person is not bombarded with multiple appeals from different parts of the institution." Eckert and Pollack (2000, p. 47) emphasized that the importance of sharing information among those faculty, staff, and administrators engaging external constituents cannot be overstated.

Cultivating and Soliciting Gifts. Just as there are some prospective donors who respond best to being cultivated and solicited by the president, there are others, particularly those in industry, who want to hear first-hand what is happening in the classrooms and labs. In this regard, the academic dean has the advantage over the president or the professional fundraising staff. Eckert and Pollack (2000) confirmed that an academic dean is often in a better position to convey what additional private support would mean to their college's programs and students, and will do so with more enthusiasm and passion than will professional fundraising staff.

NEW DIRECTIONS FOR HIGHER EDUCATION • DOI: 10.1002/he

Thanking and Recognizing Donors. A fundraising adage has it that the university can never say thank you too much. To that end, even though what will be recommended may seem repetitive of the president's donor recognition efforts, in fact by saying thank you again, the dean is reinforcing an institutional message: we appreciate your gift. Just as in the case of the president, the dean's communication should focus on the impact the donor's gift has on the academic college's programs and students. The dean should acknowledge larger gifts by phone and letter. Donald Weidner, dean of the Florida State University College of Law, says that he will "personally sign a thank you letter to every annual fund donor" (2008, p. 395). He also tries to "personally telephone every annual fund donor who contributes $500 or more." The end result, according to Weidner, is "if you give $500 to our law school's annual fund, you get a letter and a phone call from the dean."

Engaging Advisory Boards

University presidents and academic deans can enhance their fundraising efforts by creating and engaging advisory boards at all levels of the institution. For the university president, the most important advisory boards will be the governing board, foundation board, and alumni board. For academic deans, it will be college or departmental advisory boards organized to provide curricular input and a link to industry.

Members of external advisory boards should focus on (1) advocacy fostering relationships between the institution and the local, state, or regional community and industry, and increasing the profile of the university among relevant professional communities; (2) advice, assisting the president or academic dean in developing and implementing strategic plans, reviewing the effectiveness of academic programs, and serving as a sounding board for the president, academic dean, and other administrators on a variety of issues; and (3) resource development, supplying personal support, identifying prospects, opening doors, and participating in cultivation and solicitation activities.

Regardless of the number of advisory boards or at what level of the institution they operate, there should be some general coordination among these groups and the university as a whole, such as having the university president approve appointments to the boards (Flawn, 1990). The university president should also attend college or departmental advisory board meetings when possible to present informal remarks on the state of the university and attempt to relate the group's efforts to supporting the entire institution's strategic direction (Flawn, 1990).

Finding Time for Fundraising

Both the university president and the academic dean labor under enormous time pressures. Many have difficulty finding the time to do anything other than those tasks that are required of them, and sometimes not even compulsory activities find their way onto the calendar. So how is an already overscheduled president or academic dean to find time for fundraising?

Many presidents and deans shake their head or roll their eyes when they hear a fundraising consultant or other "expert" state that between 25 and 50 percent of a president or dean's time should be spent on fundraising. Even though identifying that amount of time might be unrealistic in some cases, the point is that presidents and deans need to dedicate a specific amount of time to fundraising and hold the time sacred and inviolate. Whether the president or dean sets aside three days a week or three days a month, the idea is that the professional fundraising staff will now have a specific block of time in which to schedule cultivation-and-solicitation activities. If fundraising is to be a priority for the president or dean, then it must be given appropriate attention and effort by those individuals.

Presidential time in fundraising should be spent where it is most effective and nets the greatest financial yield for the institution. Professional fundraising staff should identify the top 1 percent of institutional prospects for presidential cultivation (Slinker, 1988). The importance of spending time only where it matters most is based on the fact that the time presidents and deans spend on fundraising has significant opportunity costs—the value of not spending time on other internal and external activities on behalf of the institution or academic college.

For the reluctant fundraising president or dean, the professional fundraising staff may have to coax, pressure, or force him or her into making donor visits (Slinker, 1988). According to Slinker, this may include scheduling donor visits a president may not want to make and pursuing meetings with individuals the president may not know or like. All presidents and deans quickly come to the realization that fundraising requires time away from the office. Major gift fundraising requires house calls. Presidents and academic deans must go to a prospective donor's community, to the donor's home, office, club, or boat (Weidner, 2008). In addition to making personal visits to donors, the president and dean should set aside time to meet one-on-one and regularly with the professional fundraising staff, at least weekly but oftentimes daily.

Different from the perils of not spending enough time in fundraising are the drawbacks of spending too much time engaged in external activities. Peter Flawn, former president of the University of Texas at Austin, said, "It would be very easy for the president of the university to spend all his or her time on development work. But if you do, the institution will be managed by the vice presidents and you will lose control. You cannot abandon the internal affairs of the university to someone else and expect to be a successful president. You should maintain a firm control over both internal and external affairs" (1990, p. 166).

Working with Professional Fundraising Staff

The preceding discussion of the role of the university president and academic dean in fundraising has focused on tasks such as creating the vision, setting priorities, engaging constituents, and so on. Beyond those efforts are a large array of activities often unseen and perhaps underappreciated by the president and dean. Such is the work of the professional fundraising staff.

Olson (2006) said that faculty have an image of development staff as "glad-handers always poised for the pounce. Implicit in such negative characterizations is the belief that development activities somehow taint the purer activities of teaching and research" (p. C3). On the contrary, professional fundraising staff are a key element in ensuring the future financial viability of the lofty academic pursuits of faculty.

Professional fundraising staff have several distinct roles in a successful fundraising operation as it relates to the university president and academic dean. The first role is that of educator. Presidents and deans whose careers have been built as scholars or who have come from outside higher education are often unprepared to become fundraisers on behalf of their institution (Kaufman, 2004). Presidents with little or no experience in fundraising should look to professionals in that field for guidance and support and give those practitioners their full personal and professional confidence (Slinker, 1988). Fundraising is not as easy as it looks, and even the most experienced president or academic dean can learn from a seasoned fundraising professional.

The second role of the professional staff is that of impresario. Professional fundraising staff are responsible for organizing donor interactions between the president or academic dean so as to reflect well on the president or dean and the institution, all the while honoring the relationships between the donor and the institution. This is no easy task. It includes doing advance work such as briefing the president on the details of the visit, the background of the prospective donor, and the case for support. Advancement staff also coordinate follow-up activities after a visit by the president or dean, including preparing letters for the administrator's signature and determining when the next contact should occur.

The third role of the professional staff is that of fundraising consultant. The president or dean should work closely with development staff to set overall fundraising strategy, identify major gift prospects, and assess cultivation and solicitation opportunities around those major gift prospects. Much of successful fundraising is strategy and psychology. Collaborating with professional staff on all levels of strategy, from setting priorities to identifying prospects, will increase the potential for success of a president or dean's fundraising initiatives.

Because of the important role they play in any fundraising enterprise, care should be taken when selecting professional fundraising staff. To effectively represent the university or academic college, Weidner (2008) suggests, fundraising staff must be highly informed and capable institutional insiders. Doyle Williams, former dean of the Walton College of Business at the University of Arkansas, identifies several desired attributes of professional fundraising staff (2006): being proactive, having integrity, possessing a commitment to and knowledge of the university or academic college, using good judgment and intuition, knowing the institution's constituents, possessing fundraising expertise, and communicating well both verbally and in writing.

In the end, fundraising on behalf of the university or an academic college will be successful only if presidents, deans, and faculty recognize professional fundraising staff as their allies, not as "interlopers irrelevant to the academic enterprise" (Olson, 2006, p. C3).

Conclusion

Leadership of fundraising activities is an inescapable reality for modern university presidents and deans of academic schools and colleges. The details of their respective roles may differ slightly according to the scope of their leadership responsibilities, but the underlying commonality for both presidents and deans is that internal and external constituents expect them to lead the fundraising enterprise capably, visibly, and credibly. To do otherwise damages the institution and its ability to attract private donors to invest in the university's programs and students. Rather than being an optional activity for the president and dean, fundraising today is central to their role of institutional leader and administrator. The more presidents and deans understand and embrace that expectation, the more successful they will be as university leaders.

References

Eckert, G., and Pollack R. "Sowing the Seeds of Philanthropy." *Currents*, Sept. 2000, 26(7), 46–49.

Essex, G. L. and Ansbach, C. "Fundraising in a Changing Economy: Notes for Presidents and Trustees." *Foundation Development Abstracts*, 1993, 3(2).

Fisher, J. L. "Role of the Public College or University President in Fund Raising." In M. J. Worth (ed.), *Public College and University Development*. Washington, D.C.: Council for Advancement and Support of Education, 1985, pp. 49–56.

Flawn, P. T. *A Primer for University Presidents: Managing the Modern University*. Austin: University of Texas Press, 1990.

Glier, J. "Higher Education Leadership and Fundraising." Remarks to the Council for Industry and Higher Education. CIHE Council meeting, London, England, May 13, 2004.

Kaufman, B. "Juggling Act: Today's College or University President Must Be a Champion Fundraiser and a Strong Internal Leader." *University Business*, July 2004, 7(7), pp. 50–52.

Kvet, E. H. and Stewart, D. G. *Role of the dean in successful development*. Remarks to Development for Deans, Council for Advancement and Support of Education, February 2, 2009, Nashville, TN.

Olson, G. A. "Can You Spare a Dime?" *Chronicle of Higher Education*, May 2, 2006, p. C3.

Miller, M. T. "The College President's Role in Fund Raising. Lincoln: University of Nebraska-Lincoln." (Eric Document Reproduction Service no. ED337099), 1991.

Satterwhite, C. R. "The Function of University Presidents and CEO's in Fundraising: A Study of Public Universities with Capital Campaigns Less Than $100 Million." Unpublished doctoral dissertation, Texas Tech University, August 2004, pp. 1–177.

Sheehan, M.C. and Mihailidis, P. "Deans of Change." *American Journalism Review*, October/November 2007. Retrieved August 21, 2009, from http://www.ajr.org/ Article. asp?id=4412.

Slinker, J. M. "The Role of College or University Presidents in Institutional Advancement." Unpublished doctoral dissertation, Northern Arizona University, 1988.

Weidner, D. J. "Fundraising Tips for Deans with Intermediate Development Programs." *University of Toledo Law Review*, 2008, *39*(2), 393–398.

Williams, D. Z. "Building an Effective Fundraising Capacity." Remarks to the Canadian Federation of Business School Deans Spring 2006 conference and meeting, Vancouver, ON, June 16, 2006.

Willmer, W. K. "Blueprint for a Small College: Ten Building Blocks for Strong Advancement in Challenging Times." *Currents*, 1993, *19*(9), 36–40.

Wolverton, M., Gmelch, W. H., Montez, J., and Nies, C. T. "The Changing Nature of the Academic Deanship." Washington, D.C.: George Washington University (Eric Document Reproduction Service no. ED457708), 2001.

J. BRADFORD HODSON is the vice president for university advancement at Pittsburg State University and executive director of the PSU Foundation.

5

Evaluating the effectiveness of your fundraising program is much more than simply looking at dollars raised. Other measurements, such as number of visits, proposals submitted, effectiveness in dealing with objections, and effectiveness at managing prospects, can also help university leaders determine the success of their development programs.

Determining the Success of Fundraising Programs

Thomas S. Hiles

Every university and nonprofit in the country is interested in raising more money. Many universities spend millions of dollars to hire experienced staff, build databases, and pay for prospect travel. The question becomes, What is the return on investment? With significant and sometimes drastic budget cuts, university programs are increasingly asked to justify their existence.

As with most businesses, evaluating the effectiveness of your sales team is a function of measuring the right data. This chapter explores best practices in evaluating the effectiveness of annual and major gift teams. The chapter also looks at expectations of measuring the success of start-up programs as opposed to more established programs.

Traditional Measurements

Dollars Raised. On the surface, dollars raised would seem to be the most important way to measure effectiveness. Over time it is, and measuring dollars raised by a unit monthly or quarterly may be one of the least reliable methods of gauging productivity. The major drawback is that a university, college, or unit may receive a huge windfall through an estate gift, as an example. The current major gifts team may have done nothing to make this happen. Conversely, major gift officers may cultivate a number of important major gift prospects during a particular quarter and—whether because of the economy, a divorce, or another type of circumstance beyond their control—may not be able to close the gift.

NEW DIRECTIONS FOR HIGHER EDUCATION, no. 149, Spring 2010 © Wiley Periodicals, Inc.
Published online in Wiley InterScience (www.interscience.wiley.com) • DOI: 10.1002/he.380

Annually and beyond, measuring the growth of overall dollars raised is an important gauge. I can assure you, if your organization concentrates on proactively building relationships and engaging donors in conversation about the mutual interests of your organization and theirs, the dollars given to your organization will grow.

Number of Calls, Moves, or Contacts. Call reports are an important source of institutional memory for all nonprofit organizations. They are simply written reports of what occurred and what was learned during the donor visit. They also are used as a means to measure productivity of annual and major gift staff. Over the years, as staff grumbled about the drudgery of writing call reports, I reminded them that they not need write a Pulitzer Prize–winning document, but a good call report should share breaking news information. Obviously, a first-visit call report will need more substance than a call report on someone who has been seen many times.

Most institutions differentiate between contacts and moves. A contact is simply that; a notation is that you met a donor or talked on the phone, or perhaps sent an invitation to an event. You might find out some general information, which you would share in your call report. A move is defined as an interaction that brings you closer to closing a gift with the donor. This might be a cultivation or stewardship meeting with your president, or it might be a long-sought visit to campus.

Institutions that measure only the number of call reports entered have not begun to really measure and encourage quality strategic visits. I highlight this later in the chapter.

Proposals Submitted. A third important way in which most organizations measure productivity is by counting proposal submissions. My experience has been that proposals are an important measuring stick. After all, you can make hundreds of visits, but if you never ask, something is amiss.

Counting the number of proposals submitted by major gift officers or the number of $1,000 asks by annual fund officers is the first step. More developed programs also measure the closure rate. I talk about this as well later in the chapter.

Subjective Judgment on Measuring Quality

In talking with advancement leaders around the country, I have found that the universal question is how to measure quality solicitations. This more subjective analysis is challenging compared to counting dollars, call reports, and total number of solicitations. Here are some of the national trends.

Proposals Submitted vs. Proposals Closed. One of the most effective and simple ideas is measuring the number of solicitations by development officers (this could be major gift or annual fund officers) and gauging the number they successfully close. In a recent study by Eduventures, the average number of annual solicitations by major gifts officer was twenty-four.

The survey shared a closure rate at just under 56 percent for high-achieving programs.

This is an important statistic. In my view, a successful solicitation has a number of elements. We never want an outright *no* that hurts the relationship. A *no* can occur if you ask too quickly, or ask for the wrong amount, or for the wrong project. Development officers who take a donor-centered approach can usually avoid this response. One way is using two meetings to solicit a gift. In the first meeting you are asking for permission to solicit. The second meeting allows you personally to deliver the proposal and highlight the key selling points. Additionally, giving donors options within proposals allows more flexibility and increases your chances for success.

Dealing with Objections. Another important subjective way to measure effectiveness is by observing your development officers on calls and teaching them how to deal with donor objections. In twenty-five years in higher education advancement, I have heard just about every size and shape of objection as to why a prospect cannot give. The key is to listen and think through measurable counter ideas. This could include end-weighted gifts, stressing the need to have the donor as a role model for others, or exploring the benefits of a planned gift to avoid estate tax or create additional income.

Reading call reports and observing development officers on calls are important ways to gauge the effectiveness of your team. Strategic moves with donors require development officers to have a high social I.Q. and the ability to be an active listener. The development team should always remember that donors give big gifts for big ideas. For donors, supporting projects that transform institutions and positively affect social problems trumps a bad economy and most other donor objections.

The Call Report Audit. Early in the chapter, we touched on the importance of documenting visits and contacts with donors by using call reports. But how often are call reports used as a means to measure effectiveness? I suggest that a rather simple, but overlooked, leadership tool is to read selective call reports.

I started doing this a few years ago by asking a member of our research team to read a cross-section of the call reports made by every major gift officer and annual fund officer. From there, our researchers shared with me a small sampling of call reports from each development officer. In smaller shops, a manager could likely read most call reports online in a couple of hours.

In my division, I trust our researcher to furnish a good representation. I was surprised how much I learned about the work of my development officers from this exercise. Some make good strategic decisions on adjustments and dealing with objections during solicitations. Others make a lot of visits that do not seem to lead anywhere, and some record a call report every time they even think about a donor.

NEW DIRECTIONS FOR HIGHER EDUCATION • DOI: 10.1002/he

I was able to follow up in two ways. First, I clarified what a good call report should contain, including new information and, most important, the next steps and timeline. Additionally, I used the opportunity to discuss how to be more strategic in interaction with donors, particularly when we solicit gifts. The results of the quarterly audits were better written and effective call reports, along with more strategic donor cultivation, solicitation, and stewardship of our best prospects.

Sharing Information About Future Donor Visits

Creating a culture of sharing prospect information is an important component for a successful advancement program. It is equally important not to create excessive paperwork for the development team, who need to be on the road building relationships to support your organization.

Two strategic ways to accomplish this connection are sending bimonthly or monthly emails sharing confirmed visits and having a regular (preferable weekly) prospect discussion meeting.

Sharing Confirmed Meetings. The idea here is to recognize and encourage regular meetings between development officers and prospects. This is a very simple way for leadership to clearly see if officers are making progress. It is important to share the prospect's name and briefly describe the strategic purpose of each meeting. It is a good idea also to ask for the itinerary of each development officer before travel.

Weekly Prospect Meetings. This weekly discussion should have three ongoing agenda items:

- Discussion of proposals pending, broken down by new submissions and proposals still pending, verbal commitments, and closed proposals in writing.
- Discussion and strategy of top prospects. This can include internal rating and screening of top prospects and a discussion of next steps.
- Discussion of upcoming cultivation and donor events and other important announcements. This is the "no hiding" meeting, meaning it is an opportunity for proactive development officers to shine. If gift officers never add proposal submissions or share information on prospects, leadership needs to reinforce the priorities of the gift officer's job description.

Different Expectations for Start-up Programs vs. More Established Programs

Measuring Quality for Start-up Programs. What are the realistic performance expectations for leadership in less established programs? One of the first priorities for a new program needs to be establishing an expectation of the importance of building relationships. In fact, the two most important elements of a successful start-up program are being able to build infrastructure support while building relationships with current and future donors.

Many smaller shops or start-ups have so many issues to focus on that they forget to see donors and ask for support. Start by going on thank-you or listening tours with current donors. Evaluate effectiveness by the number of new prospects whose name you learn of during your visits.

At the same time, new programs must devote time and energy to building or expanding databases, building a basic prospect tracking and management system, and providing staff orientation and continued training. Problems occur when building the infrastructure becomes so consuming that organizations put off or even eliminate prospect visits for a period of time.

Therefore, focus on measuring programs in two areas: asking for support and building infrastructure support. Most important, departmental leaders and staff members must get out the door and build or expand relationships. They also need to ask for support by detailing how gifts will make a difference.

At the same time, you should build some infrastructure support focusing on:

- A prospect tracking and management system
- Building staff training and orientation capacity
- Create a culture of asking with a team approach

For More Established Programs. Here are some of the biggest challenges for more mature programs.

Guarding Against Complacency. Just because your organization is raising a lot of money does not mean your staff is fully productive. Drill down in looking at proposal submissions, and see how many assigned prospects never have any recorded activity on the system. Challenge your development team to always strive for continuous improvement. Leaders must be good role models and spend a significant portion of time closing leadership gifts.

Supplying Continuous Feedback. No one comes to work hoping to fail. Most of the time, struggling organizations suffer from lack of clarity about the role of each staff member. Said another way, from the point of view of each team member in the organization, "What are my most important duties? How will I be evaluated, and where do I fit on the team?" Creating clear and concise job descriptions is an important starting point. Providing continuous feedback on successes and failures is another important part of success. Too many bosses play "gotcha" at the end of the year. No one on staff should be surprised by a bad evaluation; continuous feedback is an important part of having a successful team.

Encouraging Excellence. Earlier in the chapter, we described traditional and more subjective measurement systems for gauging productivity. It is surprising how many established programs do not have the leadership asking and encouraging quality, strategic visits. This starts with the boss as a role model. Along with requiring the development team to make visits and solicit gifts, the advancement leadership team must take the lead with important donors and close important gifts.

Measuring Effectiveness

- Look at quantitative data, but drill deeper using more subjective evaluations, such as observing development officer calls and auditing the quality of call reports.
- Encourage and remind development officers that being successful requires solicitations and quality strategic planning of prospect moves. A move is any action that brings you closer to closing a gift.
- Offer clear and concise job descriptions and continuous feedback. Without clear roles, measurement systems are ineffective.
- Strive for at least a 50 percent success rate on proposal submissions. Data show that productive programs average at least a 50 percent closure rate.
- When in doubt, get out and meet with your donors. Create a culture within your team that encourages teamwork, sharing information, and shared success.

Conclusion

Remember, donors give big gifts for big ideas. At times, organizations stop asking questions about productivity if the amount of dollars raised continues going up. That is a mistake. Large estate gifts can really skew the numbers. Leaders in established programs with large campaigns need to continue asking about the closure rate on proposal submissions. They also need to look at quality visits rather than just the number of visits. Finally, leadership needs to personally observe staff intervention with donors.

With these observations and quantitative data (such as dollars raised and number of solicitations), experienced advancement leaders can measure and improve the effectiveness of their development team. Always keep in mind that donors enjoy tax deductions and naming opportunities, but transformational gifts go to organizations that demonstrate how the donor's gift will have true impact. Simply stated, donors give big gifts for big ideas.

THOMAS S. HILES *is the vice president for institutional advancement at Western Kentucky University and executive director of the WKU Foundation.*

NEW DIRECTIONS FOR HIGHER EDUCATION • DOI: 10.1002/he

This chapter describes practical steps that universities can take to more fully integrate their advancement offices to increase fundraising success. The author suggests using the for-profit integration of sales and marketing offices as a model for university action.

Integrating Development, Alumni Relations, and Marketing for Fundraising Success

Thomas R. Stevick

At many institutions, the vice president of institutional advancement oversees the functions of development, alumni relations, and marketing and communications. University leaders expect these functions to be integrated and to work hand-in-hand to advance the institution's mission, particularly in the area of private donations. The reality is that too often these three departments operate in virtual isolation, with an almost antagonistic attitude toward one another. Historic views of job responsibilities and a lack of common goals all hamper the vice president's ability to integrate these operations for full fundraising success.

Departmentally, the problem often starts at the top. Most advancement vice presidents come from a development background, with little or no experience or education in marketing or alumni relations. Development professionals might be focused on the "major gift" and "quality contacts" and not truly appreciate the impact of marketing messages or alumni programming. Likewise, alumni relations professionals may be focused on attendance at events and programs. Emphasis is placed on the number of participants, not the potential impact of the people in the room. Marketing and communication offices are populated with journalists and marketers who, unlike their counterparts in the private sector, have little responsibility for the bottom line. In an era of scarce resources, the challenge is to integrate the work of all three of these departments for the goal of increasing fundraising success.

New Directions for Higher Education, no. 149, Spring 2010 © Wiley Periodicals, Inc.
Published online in Wiley InterScience (www.interscience.wiley.com) • DOI: 10.1002/he.381

Because universities lack a tradition of this type of integration, they must look for models of integration beyond the walls of academia.

The Corporate Model: Integration of Sales and Marketing

The need to integrate the work of disparate departments to achieve revenue gain is not a problem unique to universities. For decades, the private sector dealt with the problem of the sales department and the marketing department working each in its own vacuum. In the 1990s, as competitive pressure mounted, CEOs and corporate boards demanded that "sales" and "marketing" find ways to integrate their operations and work toward common goals of revenue generation. Corporations have struggled with integration, and their internal issues associated with integration are similar to those found in university advancement operations: miscommunication due to lack of a common language, distrust resulting in failure to hand off customers at the appropriate time to maximize the sale, reward systems that recognize differing criteria of success, and battles over appropriate professional roles. The result, of course, was failure to efficiently turn leads into sales and gradual erosion of the customer base. Nevertheless, the process of integrating sales and marketing continues in the corporate world.

In addition to combining sales and marketing departments, the private sector has also developed business strategies such as customer relationship management (CRM) to ease the process of integration. CRM systems are designed to help deliver a consistent customer experience, including marketing communication, sales, and customer support. Effective CRM strategies are built on thorough, shared databases and seek to focus all employees on building and maintaining valuable relationships with prospects and customers. The results of a well-functioning CRM system include recognition of individual preferences in messaging and product, personalization of customer service, and anticipation of the customer's needs. Universities can borrow from these private sector efforts to integrate sales and marketing departments, and from the ambitions of CRM to develop strategies to more fully integrate development, alumni relations, and marketing to maximize fundraising success.

Step One: Defining Success. Corporate marketing departments were long judged on the number of leads their efforts created and the level of product awareness generated. Sales departments were judged on quarterly sales volumes. When companies began integrating these functions, they needed first to adopt a common definition of success, a common goal. The number of leads meant nothing if adequate sales were not made. Similarly, achieving short-term sales goals was not helpful if they did not build long-term, profitable relationships with the customers. Integration of sales and marketing in the private sector led to a new definition of success in these departments: to measurably acquire, grow, and retain customers. This became the common goal of the integrated "sales and marketing" department.

NEW DIRECTIONS FOR HIGHER EDUCATION • DOI: 10.1002/he

Similarly, universities must adopt definitions of success in their advancement offices that then drive integration of activities. A common definition of success would include requiring development, marketing, and alumni relations all to be responsible for identifying, cultivating, soliciting, and stewarding donors. In addition, each employee in those departments will be evaluated, in part, on his or her participation and success in these activities. Further, the entire advancement operation will be measured, and funding decisions will depend on sustained growth in private funding.

Once a straightforward definition of success is adopted, the departments can work as a team to identify the myriad ways they can integrate their work to accomplish fundraising goals: college magazine writers who consult with development professionals to emphasize private giving and private giving opportunities in their stories, bylaw requirements that all alumni advisory board members must contribute to the university, creation of teams of alumni relations officers and development staff who work together to solicit these board members, and marketing staff who train development officers on delivering carefully crafted marketing messages in one-on-one meetings with prospects. Once the advancement office understands what is meant by integration and its goals, managers in all three departments can develop work plans and strategies that fully use the capabilities of the departments.

Not all of the activities of the advancement office are necessarily aimed at fundraising. Marketing offices take on projects throughout the campus that may have only a tangential relationship to fundraising. Similarly, alumni relations offices, and even development offices, may be working with groups of constituents who have little potential for significant private support. The need will continue for this type of work in an integrated office. However, integrating for fundraising success helps focus and prioritize interactions with constituents. By adopting a common definition of success and institutionalizing the requirement of integrated fundraising activity, employees and managers in all three departments will have to consider the amount of time that is spent on each level of activity.

Step Two: Institutionalizing Integration. Corporations have responded to the need to integrate by changing corporate structure. Prior to the 1990s, there were few "Sales and Marketing" departments. The functions were separate and the employees found themselves working in silos. Corporations institutionalized integration by combining sales and marketing departments. Universities must also find ways to institutionalize the integration of advancement departments. Several ways to accomplish this are writing the goals of integration into departmental mission statements, including fundraising participation in all advancement job descriptions, and evaluating employees on their fundraising accomplishments.

Mission Statements. Advancement offices must adopt new mission statements or refine existing ones to reflect group responsibility for fundraising goals. The University of Illinois's development community has adopted a mission statement that squarely places the responsibility of revenue generating on all members of the advancement team: "The vision for advancing the University of Illinois with its key external publics is to implement an integrated development, alumni relations and marketing/communications program that will achieve strong constituent relationships and generate significant private financial resources to ensure the University's excellence" (University of Illinois Foundation, 2006, p. 4). Mission statements such as this make it clear that fundraising is a priority throughout the advancement division. From this start, the advancement vice president can design job descriptions, develop employee evaluations, and begin to create work assignments that recognize this shared goal.

Job Descriptions. Using the mission statement as a base, the advancement office should include language in job descriptions that reflects divisionwide responsibility for fundraising and long-term relationship building. The requirement to work on interdisciplinary teams to increase fundraising would be a key element of the job description. Also, the job descriptions would contain the understanding that every person employed in advancement will be required to develop and nurture long-term relationships with the goal of increasing private support for the university. Specific examples of tasks that improve fundraising results would be included in each job description. For example, the associate director in alumni relations would be required to include a fundraising component when organizing young alumni groups. Similarly, the annual fund officer will work on a team that delivers personalized institutional messages to donors that encourage continued support and build long-term connection to the institution. Each job description and work plan would include these types of requirements.

Evaluations. Similarly, job evaluations should reflect the need to integrate operations. For example, when the alumni giving participation rate begins to decrease over a period of years, advancement managers typically look to annual fund offices for answers. Is the direct mail being thrown away unopened? Have younger donors abandoned their land lines for harder-to-reach cell phones? However, in an integrated office all advancement operations would be analyzed in looking at problems such as alumni giving rate. Do alumni relations' programs encourage annual giving by those who participate? Do university marketing materials send a consistent message of participation and support? All of these efforts contribute to alumni participation and therefore should be part of an employee evaluation program. As advancement offices are integrated, the need to distribute responsibility for fundraising results will increase.

Step Three: Reinforcing Integration. Once the university has institutionalized advancement integration, the vice president must continue to reinforce the benefits of the change. Two ways to accomplish this are to furnish ongoing evidence that integration works and to enlist the backing of the university president in requiring and supporting departmental integration.

Evidence of Accomplishment. Requiring everyone in the advancement office to assume responsibility for fundraising is a big change for most

NEW DIRECTIONS FOR HIGHER EDUCATION • DOI: 10.1002/he

universities. Skeptical advancement staff members such as lifelong "journalists" or "friend raisers" may resist the effort. Even development officers who see themselves as lone wolves will have to be convinced of the power of this type of integration and collaboration. Advancement management must illustrate that specific activities of the marketing department and the alumni relations office, combined with effective solicitation, will lead directly to "sales" (gifts). One way to supply this evidence is through existing research. A number of national studies have shown that knowledgeable, involved donors are more likely to increase their donations year to year. Related studies concluded that donors who received online communications from a charity gave twice as much as donors who did not receive the same information online. A series of studies on high-net-worth donors also concluded that those who volunteer for specific events or served on charity boards gave more to organizations than those who volunteered in less significant ways. Clearly, there is evidence to tie the work of marketing (communications aimed at donors) and alumni relations (recruiting and using alumni volunteers) with fundraising results.

Advancement vice presidents must use examples like these and evidence from their own universities in creating a case for integration. Every university has a story of a board member who gave little or nothing to the university until he or she was engaged in a volunteer role and eventually became a six-, seven-, or eight-figure donor. Likewise, there is the donor who was moved by a letter from a dean or a story in the alumni magazine and set forth on the road to significant philanthropic support. Whatever form this message takes, advancement staff must be constantly reinforced with evidence that integration works.

Presidential Power. To stay competitive, corporate presidents demanded that their sales and marketing divisions begin integrating their operations. They backed up these demands by investing in technology and business processes, such as CRM systems, that allow the two functions to work together. University presidents must also insist that the traditional walls among alumni relations, development, and marketing be torn down. As the chief fundraiser, marketer, and alumni relations officer at the university, the president is in a particularly good position to expect integrated operations. After all, if the president can wear all these hats simultaneously and move effortlessly from marketer to alumni relations officer to fundraiser, then the members of the advancement office can certainly be expected to understand how to integrate their work for fundraising success. The president must also be prepared to support integration with additional resources to take full advantage of new information and communication technologies.

Step Four: Practical Steps to Integration. Advancement managers must adopt day-to-day strategies that keep integration at the forefront of their work. The first step is to create interdisciplinary teams from the marketing, development, and alumni relations departments that train and work together to address major fundraising challenges. These teams in turn will apply lessons from CRM systems to develop specific strategies and programs that build long-term relationships with donors.

Team Assignments. One strategy used by corporations is to require marketing employees to accompany sales staff on customer calls. The idea is to expose one group of employees to the other's role and begin building a common language to deal with customer demand. Similarly, field-hardened alumni relations officers and development officers can inform campus communication offices about the type of messages that alumni seek in their communications. Marketing employees can accompany them on field visits. It goes without saying that employees from marketing, development, and alumni relations should be invited to all university events where alumni and donors are presented. This gives each department an opportunity to hear the interests of its most important constituents.

Universities should also offer joint training to their advancement staff. The private sector requires marketing and sales staffs to train together to ensure consistency in messaging. Customer confusion and doubt occur when the messages in face-to-face sales meetings conflict with messages on the website or in a direct mail piece. Similarly, the entire advancement staff must be on the same page when it comes to presenting institutional information to potential donors. Whether it takes the form of an alumni e-newsletter, a press release, or a written funding proposal, the university message must be consistent. Integrated training would help the advancement staff stay current on institutional information and priorities.

Joint training and work assignments can be carried out by creating interdisciplinary teams of employees from all three departments. For example, employees can work together to form an institutional planned giving marketing effort aimed at increasing the number of donors who include the university in their estate plan. Recent studies have shown that whereas more than 50 percent of people contribute to nonprofits, only 6 percent of people have included a nonprofit in their estate plan. Further, the target audience for actually changing an estate plan is between the ages of forty and sixty. Traditionally, university marketing offices would help the planned giving office develop brochures and newsletters, but the messaging and the responsibility for success would all be on the shoulders of the planned giving officer. Instead, what if an interdisciplinary team of marketers, alumni relations officers, and development professionals all were responsible for the success of landing new estate commitments? Marketing would bring its experience in developing messages that reach the target age group. Alumni relations would use its network of clubs and events to encourage participation. Development officers would deliver passionate and succinct communications about the university that were developed by the marketing team and aimed at influencing donors to include the university in their estate plans. In these ways, integrated teams would contribute to fundraising success.

Applying CRM. Once interdisciplinary teams are created, advancement offices can use the lessons from CRM applications to create a personalized relationship with donors. Corporations have used CRM strategy to move from mass marketing to customer-centric marketing. CRM also allows businesses to be proactive in anticipating customers' needs instead of waiting for the customer to call. All of this is built on a base of shared data and the use of burgeoning communication technology. The goal, of course, is to build long-term, satisfied customers. CRM should not be seen merely as a technology; many universities already have the technology needed to accomplish these goals. Instead it should be viewed as a customer-centered approach that leverages integrated work teams, data, and communication technology.

Our advancement offices have the same goals as most businesses: satisfied long-term constituents who regularly support our operations. Unlike businesses, universities have yet to fully integrate their advancement operations and use strategies such as CRM to personalize their relationships with donors. An integrated office would develop ways to individualize communications with donors. The same, easy-to-use database would track marketing messages, event attendance and visits to campus, areas of support, solicitations, call-ins and complaints, and the donors' personal interests. Although databases like these exist on university campuses, they are not used to their full potential to create and maintain long-term relationships.

Further applying CRM strategies, the advancement office would personalize not only communication but also solicitation and stewardship efforts. By tracking the donor's interests and areas of support, advancement offices can be proactive in invitations to campus events and targeted about their solicitation efforts. The explosion in advanced communication technology offers even more opportunities to pinpoint relevant information to share with specific donors and maintain the type of long-term, relevant relationship that leads to fundraising success.

Conclusion

University advancement offices and corporate sales and marketing offices are facing many of the same issues today. Cold calls are becoming less and less effective. Sales people and development officers all report increased difficulty in getting quality appointments. Direct mail, telephone centers, and email campaigns all struggle for success as privacy managers and information overload affect how donors and customers receive messages.

Decades ago, private industry responded to these trends by beginning to integrate the sales and marketing functions to more succinctly communicate with their customers and deliver personalized, proactive service. This continues to be an ongoing process in the corporate world, and products and strategies such as CRM have been developed to assist in creating long-term relationships with customers, with the ultimate goal of increased revenue.

University advancement offices must begin integrating departments and activities for the purpose of increasing private donations. This begins by

NEW DIRECTIONS FOR HIGHER EDUCATION • DOI: 10.1002/he

vesting the entire operation with the responsibility to identify, cultivate, steward, and solicit donors. Precisely how each member of the advancement team can contribute must be spelled out in a job description and employee evaluation, and interdisciplinary teams need to be created to design ways in which each department can participate in major fundraising initiatives. Finally, university leadership must continue to support integration and encourage its growth through resource allocation. By using the corporate model of integration between sales and marketing, university advancement offices can take some concrete steps and integrate their own operations for fundraising success.

Reference

University of Illinois Foundation. *Strategic Plan for Development: Facilitating a brilliant future for the University of Illinois.* Retrieved Jan. 25, 2010, from http://www.uillinois. edu/strategicplan/plans/UIF%20Developmemt_Strategic_Plan_1-6-06.pdf.

Thomas R. Stevick is the vice president for university advancement at Ohio Northern University.

NEW DIRECTIONS FOR HIGHER EDUCATION • DOI: 10.1002/he

7

Fundraising for both academic purposes and intercollegiate athletics presents challenges that must be recognized.

Balancing Fundraising in Academic Programs and Intercollegiate Athletics

Elizabeth H. King, Eric L. Sexton, James J. Rhatigan

There is an uneasy relationship between fundraising for academic programs and intercollegiate athletics. This has little to do with individuals and almost everything to do with circumstances in higher education in the United States that have come into play in recent decades. This chapter identifies issues presidents will confront as they seek funds for academic programs and intercollegiate sports. In spite of difficulties, models for successful practice do exist. Two prevailing models are noted, along with some illustrations of good practice.

The Role of Intercollegiate Athletics in Fundraising

There is no question as to who is winning the competition for control of intercollegiate athletics. Television revenue represents the most significant source of fundraising for intercollegiate sports. Big-time college sports clearly are in the entertainment business. Athletic conferences today are making their own financial arrangements, and even individual schools with high visibility are entering into contracts. Commerce is the underpinning, as advertising revenue supplies the wherewithal for television to offer its vast sums, the key to funding intercollegiate sports.

The NCAA still stands for institutional control, but its insistence seems pale, and its hold tenuous, when hundreds of millions of dollars are at stake. At the highest levels of competition in two sports, men's basketball and men's football, coaches trump presidents. The most successful coaches, who likely are tremendous fundraisers, command long-term contracts with

NEW DIRECTIONS FOR HIGHER EDUCATION, no. 149, Spring 2010 © Wiley Periodicals, Inc.
Published online in Wiley InterScience (www.interscience.wiley.com) • DOI: 10.1002/he.382

healthy buy-out features and enjoy salary benefits in multiple figures beyond that of the president. Salaries of assistant coaches now may reach six figures in these sports. Some earn a salary nearly equivalent to that of the president. Sports manufacturers have become a part of the fundraising story as they provide equipment and cash to coaches.

Winning dominates all other factors. Consider the coach with an exemplary reputation who is loved and respected as a teacher by his or her players, whose only flaw is a losing record. If the words "consistently losing" arise, this coach in NCAA Division 1 (and Division 1-A) sports will not survive. It is a rare president who could save such a coach, and an even rarer one who would try. Alumni and students expect to win. Winning costs money, and successful fundraising in intercollegiate athletics equates to winning.

If one moves down the hierarchical (NCAA) ladder, the perks and the problems may differ, but they still exist. Financial issues in lower categories of intercollegiate competition do not disappear. Women's sports are now in the mix, particularly basketball, volleyball, and soccer. They are developing larger fan bases, and this outcome commands money. Some of this fan base is new, but more likely there is considerable overlap as fundraisers pursue available dollars.

It is encouraging that well-informed and dedicated donors are still committed to the "love of the game" and are looking for ways to effectively support their favorite programs. It would be naïve, however, to think that the institution freely reciprocates this support. Philanthropic dollars may determine exactly where fans sit! Loyalty is not determined by lengthening years, through good years and bad. Today, premier seating and other benefits carry a price tag.

In the United States, the accident of history has produced this unintended, sprawling, highly successful entertainment business. It would seem difficult to make the case that college sports have an academic underpinning, but there is room for argument.

Successful college coaches are excellent teachers and motivators. It takes good intelligence for players to participate effectively. Some important corollary skills also surface (such as teamwork and discipline). Individual and team failures, for example, have to be dealt with immediately as a team prepares for its next contest. It may well be that important elements such as these are transferable to life after college. Most people see the importance of practice, preparation, and persistence in successful outcomes. Studies have indicated a disproportionate degree of success on the part of those who were able to compete in intercollegiate supports. The professoriate should not ignore the successful teaching that occurs in intercollegiate sports. Donors feel, very directly, that they are helping students through their support.

University presidents certainly would regard sports teams as a leading source of donor entertainment. Though it may not be fair, some people will see the success of an institution as grounded in athletics. When Wichita State University gave up football in 1987, after years of financial drain and poor fan support, at first it was unsettling. How could there be an institution without football? There is ongoing conversation about when it will return. However, many people feel that all of the other sports at Wichita State actually have prospered from the change.

It is common to read about sports as the "front door" of the university. Conversation around the watercooler will always focus on sports rather than the substantive academic work that goes on in a university. Why? Sports in America are the national pastime. Competitive team sports begin with five-year-olds and intensify at every level along the way. Individual sports (such as golf and tennis) have huge followings and their own heroes. When people can no longer play, they watch. This has financial implications. Gender, age, race: it really doesn't matter. Intercollegiate sports are understandably embedded in this culture.

There is less agreement about whether successful athletics support academic fundraising. Lombardi and others (2003) surveyed the literature and were not convinced of the connection. In addition, Frey (1985), Gerdy (2002), Zimbalist (1999, 2000), and Staurowsky (1996) studied the relationship between intercollegiate athletics and higher education, all concluding there is little empirical support for the notion that athletic success translates to academic fundraising support. It does seem incontrovertible that intercollegiate sports serve a role in sustaining alumni interests, and that fan loyalty and institutional loyalty seem indistinguishable at times. Incidental giving to the academy may accompany contributions to sports, and certainly there is evidence that on occasion large dollars come to the academic side of the enterprise from donors whose initial giving was to sports. T. Boone Pickens's generosity to Oklahoma State University is a current example. The potential for greater financial reciprocity between athletics and academics does represent an exciting challenge.

Fundraising for Academic Programs

The general public in recent years has seemed frustrated with the inability of institutions to cooperate with each other. Higher education is not exempt. Select any urban area in the nation and you will find many higher educational institutions seeking support. All of them are capable of producing intelligent, appropriate, and compelling stories that will tug at business leaders and individual philanthropists who want to do their share for the common good in their immediate world. Many of these potential donors never attended the institutions they are asked to support. Competition for resources in higher education is civil, but this does not lessen its intensity.

Even single institutions face issues of cooperation and collaboration in fundraising. This may produce wasted time and energy, and generate conflict. The playing field is no longer neutral. It may come down to funding an expensive academic journal or getting better seating at athletic events. Challenges are growing as financial needs within an institution increase. In fact, within a twelve-month period a potential donor on a single campus may hear from the Alumni Association, the Athletic Department, Library Associates, the Art Museum, the Annual Fund of the Foundation, development officers in the Foundation, an academic college, even a department. Add to this list specific enthusiasms a donor is known to support, such as golf tournaments, auctions, and support groups. These areas, of course, are not located in a single reporting structure. Taken together, these elements need careful management. Otherwise donors will complain, and some of these complaints will be expressed directly to the president. When this happens, the president will respond! If it happens often, there will be consequences.

Institutions are always in the process of expanding their donor pool, but in the short run the pool tends to be flat. It is a possibility that a donor will receive more than one contact from an institution. During a time of recession, this issue is more apt to surface because wealthy donors are increasingly anxious. Their net worth has been hard hit, but of greater consequence are the reduced dividends that have adversely affected giving capacity. Even as the economic situation begins to improve, it will be a challenge to overcome the negative psychology introduced into the lives of these donors.

The idea of serenity in academic fundraising today seems quaint indeed. Foundations have recovered only slightly from the financial crisis in the current economy. Virtually all public institutions have lost substantial state support. In instances where financial support for academic affairs is suffering and athletics are growing, tensions are inevitable. On selected campuses, faculty are openly expressing concerns about unfilled vacant positions, lack of pay increases, possible furloughs, deferred maintenance, and equipment shortfalls for library and laboratory, while intercollegiate sports seem to be immune (Wieberg, Upton, Perez, and Berkowitz, 2009). Yet there has never been a time in the history of the United States when giving to support academic projects equals that of the present day. A persuasive argument could be made that presidents are the reason. The situation is ideal when fundraising for academic affairs and intercollegiate sports are part of the executive agenda. There might be idiosyncratic reasons for fundraising success on a campus, but more likely they fall into one of two models.

Model One: Centralized Approach. A *centralized approach*, as seen in Table 7.1, is characterized by having the foundation as the entity responsible for all fundraising. Athletic fundraising in this model is a component part of the overall effort and is considered on par with the academic colleges. The goals for fundraising are developed through the foundation in cooperation with the academic colleges; fundraising staff throughout the campus report to the foundation president or CEO.

In this model, athletic fundraisers are treated in the same manner as all other development officers on the foundation staff. These officers serve in a dotted-line relationship with their respective areas. They share information and training and are in a position to help one another. The major gifts

Table 7.1 Centralized Approach

	Foundation	Athletics
Pros	Clear donor management and coordination	Ability to have more development professionals working on athletic needs
	Ability to manage entire fundraising landscape	Closer ties with athletic programs and staff
Cons	Athletic interests may overshadow academic interests	Athletics not necessarily the top priority for foundation goals
	Lack of clarity	Lack of control

person in athletics is required to coordinate all work with donors as a part of a prospect management strategy by clearing and reporting all contacts. There are a number of positive and negative features to this more centralized approach to fundraising.

Model Two: Decentralized Approach. An alternative model that also can be effective has athletic fundraising as part of the intercollegiate athletic department. In this *decentralized approach* (see Table 7.2), the athletic fundraisers report directly to the athletic director and coordinate all efforts with the foundation. As an example, the athletic department fundraising staff might attend all foundation prospect management meetings as well as work directly with foundation staff on all gift agreements and donor acknowledgments. Athletic fundraising staff members in this model work specifically on annual, planned, and major gift campaigns to achieve departmental goals. Athletics has the responsibility to cultivate, steward, and acquire gifts on behalf of the athletic department in accordance with the standards set by the foundation. Depending on the institution, this approach will still have strong ties to the foundation in the areas of donor records and similar important recordkeeping functions. There are other attractive opportunities to creatively package proposals, merging academic and athletic interests to meet the goals of prospects. The decentralized model, of course, has its own pros and cons.

Best Practices

The literature clearly reveals lack of connection between athletic and academic fundraising. Attention probably should be paid, however, to the celebrity role that athletics brings to the fundraising effort. Successful, high-profile coaches do give fundraising campaigns some beneficial star power, which is very beneficial. Joe Paterno, the current football coach at Penn State, illustrates how success in intercollegiate athletics may generalize. Coach Paterno has given some of his own wealth to the institution and helped raise money for academic projects. Has his behavior inspired others?

Table 7.2 Decentralized Approach

	Foundation	Athletics
Pros	Workload responsibilities are clearly delineated	Staff are dedicated to athletic fundraising and understand athletics
		Staff can be involved in additional athletic efforts: sport team management, etc.
Cons	May foster unnecessary and unproductive competition	Risk lack of coordination with foundation
	Loss of control	Not always included in overall fundraising goals
		Athletics development staff can be distracted with competing projects and not focus just on fundraising

One would expect former players who go on to success in the world to demonstrate behavior consistent with that of their beloved coach. Other successful coaches have likewise been able to help their institutions.

Urban Meyers and Billy Donovan, two successful coaches at the University of Florida, are heading an effort to raise $50 million in need-based scholarships for first-generation students (Brazda, 2008). Their coaching success has made this possible, and they are outstanding examples of the meaning of cooperation, demonstrating the ability of coaches to make an impact on academic fundraising.

The University of Kansas is currently engaged in expansion of its football stadium, with a collateral goal of making $40 million available for academic use at the university. Here we see how extension of an athletic project benefits the larger institution.

A couple in the process of making a large estate gift for the art collection at Wichita State University mentioned the female partner had played tennis in college years ago. Learning that the women's tennis program was poorly funded, the couple made a gift to support the program. This illustrates how an academic development officer with a good ear may have an opportunity to support athletics.

A couple considering gifts to create chairs in anesthesia and urology (the medical specialties of these two physicians) were planning to attend a bowl game in which the University of Iowa was a participant (email message from L. Marshall to E. H. King, Sept. 24, 2009). They were invited to attend a practice session, where they met the orthopedist who was the team physician. Soon the head coach stopped by, visited, and posed for pictures. The two doctors were enthralled, according to reports, and in a matter of days they completed a gift agreement for several million dollars. Even small gestures can have positive consequences. This kind of institutional cooperation cannot be scripted but instead is a matter of mutuality.

Conclusion

There are several windows for the university to offer opportunities to connect donors, boosters, alumni, and others to their institution. It is important to make these constituency relationships as positive as possible to meet the goals. The conventional wisdom fosters a tension between the athletic and academic units with respect to fundraising. It would be naïve to ignore such observations, but they can be overcome through institutionwide perspectives and organizational arrangements that foster cooperation.

References

Brazda, C. "Billy Donovan and Urban Meyer to Lead Drive to Raise $50 Million Florida Opportunity Scholars Program." (News release.) University of Florida Foundation, Oct. 14, 2008.

Frey, J. "The Winning-Team Myth." *Currents*, Jan. 1985, 16(1), 33–35.

Gerdy, J. *Sports: The All-American Addiction*. Jackson: University Press of Mississippi, 2002.

Lombardi, J. V., Craig, D. D., Capaldi, E. D., Gater, D. S., and Rivers, D. "The Top American Research Universities." *Annual report of the Lombardi Program on Measuring University Performance*. Gainesville: University of Florida, 2003.

Staurowsky, E. J. "Women and Athletic Fundraising: Exploring the Relationship Between Gender and Giving." *Journal of Sports Management*, Oct. 1996, 401–416.

Wieberg, J., Upton, J., Perez, A. J., and Berkowitz, S. "At Many Colleges, Education Takes Hit But Athletics Budgets Continue to Grow in Recession." *USA Today*, Nov. 10, 2009, A1–A2.

Zimbalist, A. *Unpaid Professionals: Commercialism and Conflict in Bigtime College Sports*. Princeton, N.J.: Princeton University Press, 1999.

Zimbalist, A. "Academics Get No Boost from Booster; Study Fails to Link Athletic Success to Rise in University Wide Gifts." *Street and Smith Sports Business Journal*, Sept. 4–10, 2000, p. 52.

ELIZABETH H. KING *is the president and CEO of the Wichita State University Foundation.*

ERIC L. SEXTON *is the director of athletics at Wichita State University.*

JAMES J. RHATIGAN *is a retired Wichita State University vice president, working as a consultant for the Wichita State University Foundation.*

NEW DIRECTIONS FOR HIGHER EDUCATION • DOI: 10.1002/he

8

This chapter gives an overview of systems used in support of the art of fundraising through strategic development of prospective donors into donors.

Prospect Development Systems: Empowering Artful Fundraising

By Dan J. Nicoson

"Donors don't give to causes; they give to people with causes." This often-cited saying rings true and emphasizes that the donor is influenced largely by the personality, professionalism, and character of the asker. The interpersonal skills of development officers and key volunteers are critical to development of relationships with donors, a fact that cannot be overemphasized. Applying these skills is the art of fundraising. This notwithstanding, the science and systems of fundraising give the development officer the information tools to be applied in practicing this art. This chapter focuses on the systems and processes supporting development of constituents as prospects, and ultimately as donors.

Qualifying Prospects

It is simply not feasible to develop a personal relationship with every constituent of the university. This would require more staff and resources than it is possible to mobilize. Even if such resources were available, it would be inefficient and irresponsible to commit them to constituents who will not become major donors. Without a system to identify those constituents most likely to become valid prospects, the development staff might as well affix a list of constituents to a bulletin board and throw darts to determine which ones are to be the subject of their efforts.

To maximize the efficiency and productivity of the development staff, there must be an investment in a system to qualify constituents as prospects. The Fundraising School at the Indiana University Center on Philanthropy

NEW DIRECTIONS FOR HIGHER EDUCATION, no. 149, Spring 2010 © Wiley Periodicals, Inc.
Published online in Wiley InterScience (www.interscience.wiley.com) • DOI: 10.1002/he.383

teaches the principle of LAI (linkage, ability, and interest) as the qualifying factors of valid prospects. This system confirms the constituents' relationship with the university and the financial capability to give, and it assesses their level of interest in the university. Relying on various available methods of gathering facts about prospects, this system is collectively known as prospect research. These methods are units of study in themselves, but it suffices here to briefly mention some examples.

Electronic Screening. Vendors contract to screen all or part of your roster of constituents against national models, or a model from your own database of past donors. A report is generated that rates the constituents in various categories to help the development staff determine which constituents appear to be the better prospects. There is a margin of error in a mass process of this type, but it is far better than throwing darts, and it is a guide to which constituents should be the focus of additional research.

Review of Internal Data. A review of in-house records pertaining to past donors and nondonor constituents yields helpful information. Alumni records can tell you the age, area of study, job titles, extracurricular activities, and events attended since graduation. This information helps the staff better know the alum. "The best prospects are past donors" is another cardinal principle of fundraising. University donor records tell which constituents have already shown an interest by making contributions, how much was given, and the type of appeal to which the constituents responded.

Peer Evaluations. Individuals close to universities and their development staffs are often in a position to have knowledge about other constituents. They might be recruited to review the list of constituents and supply information that is helpful in estimating constituents' ability to give, determining centers of influence, and predicting what might motivate them to become donors.

Advanced Prospect Research. The preceding examples are forms of prospect research. The presence of prospect research specialists on the development staff allows these processes to be conducted by prospect researchers, instead of drawing time away from the important work of development officers with prospects. These prospect researchers can also further the process of obtaining important information through use of online databases and other research techniques. The product of their work is identification of valid prospects and briefs given to development officers as tools for their use in practicing their art.

Developing the Cultivation Plan

Once someone is qualified as a prospect for substantial giving, the development officer will treat development of the prospect as a campaign in and of itself. This individual campaign addresses what is to be done to move the prospect from point A (the person's current relationship) to point B (ready to become a donor).

NEW DIRECTIONS FOR HIGHER EDUCATION • DOI: 10.1002/he

This process involves strategic use of telephone contacts, correspondence, special events, tailored activities, and personal visitations. Some take exception with the term "moves management," but Bill Sturtevant (1997) presents excellent information in his writings on this subject. He explains the objectives of strategic moves, and their role in the process. These strategic steps are complemented by general contacts such as newsletters, greeting cards, annual reports, and other forms of communication.

The "ask" for the contribution comes at the end of the strategic campaign. There are various publications available on the process of making the ask (some are listed at the end of this chapter), for study by development officers. It serves us well, however, to think of the entire strategic process as one of asking for the contribution. The Fundraising School at the Indiana University Center on Philanthropy teaches four parts to asking for a contribution: the opening, involvement, presentation, and the close. These four parts should be considered throughout execution of the planned strategy for development of the prospect.

The first goal of the process, which is addressed in the opening, is to help the prospect develop a comfort level and rapport with the development officer and key volunteer. This increases the likelihood of the prospect being willing to accept staff calls, visits, and invitations. Involvement is an opportunity for the prospect to share information about perceptions of the institution and what is important to her or him about the institution. This information can guide needed adjustment in the planned strategies. In the presentation phase, the development staff or volunteer takes greater control of the process to present information pertaining to the importance of what it is for which support is sought. The close is an overt attempt to gain confirmation of the support that is sought.

It is important that the prospect's thinking be understood as early in the process as possible. Prince and File (1994) describe seven types of donors, their motivations and idiosyncrasies, and general types of approaches to each type. Whether using these seven categories or ones developed by the development officer, before an individual strategy is initiated the staff makes judgments about the characteristics of the donor and plans an individual strategy accordingly. However, it is essential that the staff remain flexible and make adjustments to perceptions of the prospect and the strategies to be used as new information is acquired.

Assigning Prospects

The strategic plan pertaining to a specific prospect is led and coordinated by a development officer to whom the prospect is assigned. In a small development office there may be only one option or a few, but at institutions with a larger development staff there might be various factors helping to determine to which member of the staff a prospect is assigned. This may be decided by the geographical location in which the prospect resides, or by the academic

NEW DIRECTIONS FOR HIGHER EDUCATION • DOI: 10.1002/he

unit with which the prospect is considered to have affinity. The assignment might be made on the basis of which development officer is considered to have the best personality match with the prospect. However the assignment is determined, this development officer coordinates contacts from the university, involvement of volunteers, issuing of special invitations, and other "strategic moves."

One organizational model I favored is that used at Bowling Green State University (BGSU), overseen by Marcia Latta, vice president of the Bowling Green State University Foundation. The BGSU major gifts program is a centralized one in which major gift officers are within the development office, report to the vice president, and are assigned to geographical regions each with a concentration of university constituents. Each major gifts officer is also assigned as a liaison with specific academic units or programs within the university. They are charged with keeping abreast of the needs and goals of these units and seeing that the entire major gifts staff is aware of them.

Executing the Plan

At this point the prospect has been qualified, strategic goals and plans have been determined, and a specific member of staff has been assigned to coordinate execution of the planned strategy. It is now time to execute this strategy and move steadily toward successful conclusion.

Execution of the plan is a dynamic process that must be approached with flexibility. As the strategy is carried out, some prospects may be dropped from the process because information is obtained that disqualifies the subject as a valid prospect. Other information may become known that alters the anticipated timeline of the strategy, the specific volunteers who should be involved, the events to which the prospect will be invited, or even the purpose for which the gift is solicited. Lack of flexibility on these matters could well prevent this individual campaign from reaching the desired outcome.

This development of a desired relationship and closure of the gift is generally not a quick process. The required timeline is commonly said to be eighteen to thirty months, and sometimes longer. This being the case, a development staff that experiences a high rate of turnover is at a disadvantage because the process of developing the relationship may be interrupted.

Involvement of university or program leadership may be an important part of the strategic process. Remembering that donors give to people with a cause, prospective donors often feel it is the top leadership in whom they are investing. Thus the involvement of the university president, or other key leadership, should be carefully considered in developing the strategy. These leaders, especially the president, should be used much as a football team uses a star running back. They should not be overused, but when the crucial play is needed the ball is placed in the hands of the star.

Conclusion

The objective of the strategic process is to reach the point at which the linkage, ability, and interest are all in place and it is deemed appropriate to make the ask for the contribution. As the strategy is executed and adjustments are made to move the process forward, the development team is looking for the right circumstances to ask for the gift. Once this time has arrived, care should be taken to select the best person to make the ask. The general rule is that the best person is a peer of the prospect, usually a volunteer rather than a member of the staff. However, I believe donors are more sophisticated than they once were and more accustomed to working with professional representatives, whether the president, the development officer, or another key person. Again, the overall objective is to get the right person to ask the right prospect for the right gift at the right time.

The heart of obtaining closure is asking for the contribution. Here are some points to keep in mind as the development officer develops the art of asking:

- Anticipate objections that the prospect will have, and attempt to answer them prior to the ask.
- The asking process may or may not be completed in a single visit. The four parts of the ask mentioned earlier must be played out even if it takes more than one visit.
- The development officer must be herself or himself. After rapport has been developed, the prospect will sense a change in personality. The development officer must determine what techniques work best for her or him. For example, I have found that prospects expect the ask, and I am very candid and direct in making it.
- The manner in which the ask is made should be such that even a negative response leaves open a continued relationship and further discussion.

It is important to realize that the goal of this entire prospect development system is to develop the appropriate relationship with prospects, not to manipulate them. A donor with whom a proper relationship has been developed experiences personal satisfaction from making something significant happen at the university. She or he is appreciative of the relationship with the university and the development staff. This leads to a continued relationship that may result in additional investments in the future.

Figure 8.1 is a flow chart of the excellent prospect development system used by Brad Hodson, vice president for university advancement at Pittsburg State University in Kansas, and his development staff. It illustrates several important points:

Figure 8.1. Excellent Prospect Development System Flow Chart

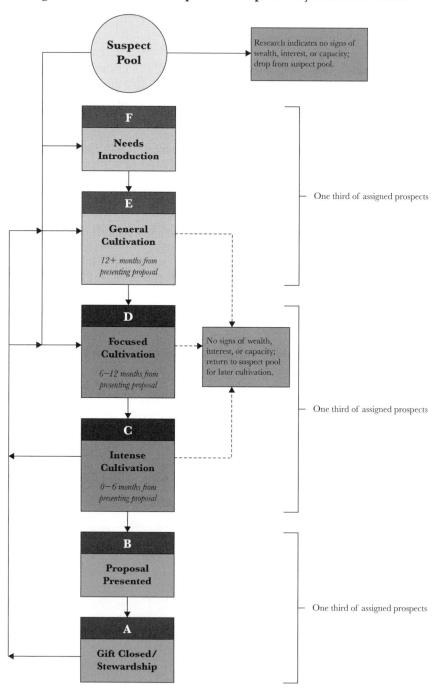

- Note that the flow chart shows prospects removed from the process and returned to the "suspect pool" during the cultivation activities (levels E, D, and C) if information is obtained that disqualifies the prospect. This is the flexibility that was mentioned previously.
- The timeline estimates level E to be twelve months prior to proposing the gift, level D is six to twelve months prior, and level C is up to six months prior. Again, flexibility is required as the process progresses with each prospect.
- It is anticipated that approximately one-third of the assigned prospects will be at levels F and E, one-third at levels D and C, and one-third at levels B and A.
- The arrows to the left of levels C and A indicate that the prospect is returned to level E or D. This acknowledges that they do not return to the suspect pool or level F because they have already been qualified. Return to E or D after C simply represents that something occurred at level C to believe a proposal is not yet in order, and continued attention to the prospect is advised. Returning to E or D after level A acknowledges that past donors are the best prospects, and this donor's gift does not represent the end of the process.

References

Prince, R. A., and File, K. M. *The Seven Faces of Philanthropy*. San Francisco: Jossey-Bass, 1994.

Sturtevant, W. *The Artful Journey: Cultivating and Soliciting the Major Gift*. Chicago: Bonus Books, 1997.

DAN J. NICOSON is vice president for university advancement at Missouri Western State University, executive director of the Missouri Western State University Foundation, and a member of the adjunct faculty at the Indiana University Center on Philanthropy, the Fundraising School.

This chapter offers thoughts on some key elements of a high-performing development environment.

Recruiting, Training, and Retaining High-Performance Development Teams

Stephen D. Elder

When we rolled out our campaign strategy in a development team retreat, my staff was surprised to see me ride in on a unicycle with country music blaring. After zigzagging among them, I got off and told them the story of learning to ride when I was a kid.

The morning of the retreat, I had pulled it out of the closet and dusted it off for a little ride. Why?

It takes three big things to learn to ride a unicycle: practice, falling, and balance. You have to practice (a lot). You have to risk falling (often). You are seeking balance (in all things).

As a team, we were being asked by President Dick Celeste and Colorado College to take on huge fundraising goals. We knew that to get different results, we were going to have to do things differently. In this new way of thinking—which we came to call a "just ask" culture—we knew we were going to have to fail, learn, fail again, learn, and eventually find balance. In so doing, we would build a strong team around this new approach.

I was giving them permission to fail.

Over the six years since that first retreat, we have learned a great deal together. It is a privilege to be able to share with you some of the things we have learned. This chapter houses a menagerie of metaphors. Metaphors are powerful teaching and communication tools. For this chapter, it was tempting to try to make them consistent for editorial purposes. Instead, I have chosen to use them as they are naturally (and somewhat randomly) invoked in day-to-day management.

New Directions for Higher Education, no. 149, Spring 2010 © Wiley Periodicals, Inc.
Published online in Wiley InterScience (www.interscience.wiley.com) • DOI: 10.1002/he.384

A word about terms and titles: for this chapter, I use the terms *development officer, major gift officer*, and *director of development* interchangeably when speaking about field-deployed fundraisers, the core of an effective development team.

Set a Compelling Vision with Big Goals

People love to be part of something big, something that transforms a place and its people. Change the world. Leave a legacy. Good development officers are especially wired that way. Ask them to take a quantum leap, and they will lead the way.

Dick Celeste (who rides a Segway as *his* campus vehicle of choice), in his first year as president, led a strategic planning process that mapped out a collective vision for the future of the college. The "cost" of realizing and sustaining the vision was around $300 million—about twice what traditional approaches would have determined should be our campaign goal. But it was the vision that compelled and focused us, not dollar totals set by asking "what we think we can raise." There was never any question about the college's potential.

Thinking big is a powerful concept for development officers. Thinking big is a lot easier than being mediocre. It is easier to ask someone for big dollars for a big idea (assuming they have the financial capacity) than it is to ask someone with relatively little money for $1,000. Steve Jobs, founder of Apple, is widely quoted as saying, "I want to put a ding in the universe."

Be Clear About Priorities

Clear means simple. Our development priorities are the three things it takes to have a great college: faculty, students, and campus. We have a lot of good language around those things and lots of projects to fund—scholarships, professorships, and buildings—but in the end we raise money for those three things. Everything we do leads to investment in these three interrelated circles. Fortunately, most committed and generous investors care the most about those three things!

Give Your Team the Training and the Tools They Need for Success

Your vision and goals are your fundraisers' most important tools. They not only motivate development officers, they inspire investors. But your team needs more. Development officers need specific training and regular practice in a relationship-based sales process. Yes, I used the *S* word. In essence, colleges and universities are asking development officers to be frontline salespeople. If we do not give them the training and tools these salespeople need they will not be successful, they will become frustrated, and they will leave (or worse, become frustrated, unmotivated, and *stay*).

The centerpiece of our training is a presentation piece, a framework for development officers to tell the story of the vision, priorities, and plan for the campaign and how investors can help advance it. Our officers can give this presentation to anyone in any situation, and they do. They don't have to "prequalify" each person they meet with. They don't have to invent a strategy for each prospect, project, or visit. Their goal is to make the presentation as many times as possible, and the goal of the presentation is for the potential investor to ask, "How can I help?"

All elite teams have one thing in common: practice. How often does your development team practice its presentations? How often do the team members use the dreaded role play? Do they honestly break down their visits and share what they are learning? Michael Gelb, Zen master of the learning organization, says, "Your awareness of the gap between a goal you passionately want to reach and an accurate assessment of your present status creates tension. The willingness to embrace this tension with a positive attitude is a distinguishing feature of the most effective learners" (2003, p. 15).

You Get What You Measure

Good development officers like their work to be measured. They are competitive, sure, but mostly they want to get better, make an impact, and be successful. Gelb talks about an "accelerated learning spiral," with two key ingredients: "1) a vivid visualization of success based on a model of excellence, and 2) accurate feedback on your performance. Both ingredients are essential. If you have a clear vision but inaccurate feedback, you will be deluded, living in a fantasy world. If you have accurate feedback but are without vision, you will be uninspired and stagnant" (2003, p. 17).

To help inspire our team, we measure how many visits they make, how many other contacts they have with qualified prospects, how many asks and presentations they are completing, how many legacy (estate) conversations they are having, what their prospects are doing with their annual giving, and total dollar commitments in each category. They report all of these actual results against "good, better, and best" goal categories for each activity that they have designed for themselves, working with managers. Then we discuss in detail their results, which failures they are learning from, and which victories they are enjoying.

Funding guru Tom Suddes says, "Sales requires measurement. The old adage of 'what gets measured gets done' is an overused/abused cliché, but it captures the essence of a SALES culture. EVERYTHING, and I mean EVERYTHING, needs to be MEASURED. Activity/Productivity. What works/What doesn't. Every number/every project" (2006, p. 39).

Jim Collins, author of the famous *Good to Great: Why Some Companies Make the Leap . . . and Others Don't* (2001), advises what he calls "social sector organizations" this way: "It doesn't really matter whether you can quantify your results. What matters is that you rigorously assemble *evidence*—quantitative or qualitative—to track your progress. If the evidence is primarily qualitative, think like a trial lawyer assembling the combined body of evidence. If the evidence is primarily quantitative, then think of yourself as a laboratory scientist assembling and assessing the data" (2005, p. 7).

I wonder how many balls Tiger Woods has hit in his lifetime. I would bet he could tell us.

Create a Coaching Environment

Good players love to improve their game, so they appreciate good coaching. The same is true of good development officers. I learned this from Tom Suddes, our "nonconsultant campaign coach." Among many other things, Suddes has coached the Notre Dame boxing team for more than thirty years. To our team, he brought an authentic, direct, and motivating coaching style. He does not pull punches. He coaches the "whole person." He has helped us create a coaching environment that works in all directions; we all coach each other, and we have fun doing it!

Suddes introduced us to many of the ideas, sources, and concepts in this article, and a lot more. By example, he teaches that illuminating our failures is an important element of an authentic learning and coaching environment.

Get the Right Players on the Field

Jim Collins stresses the importance of "getting the right people on the bus within social sector constraints." He says, "A finding from our research is instructive: the key variable is not how (or how much) you pay, but *who* you have on the bus" (2005, p. 15).

Collins contrasts the companies that tried to motivate their workers by emphasizing incentives to those "great" companies that focused on recruiting and retaining the "right" people. He describes his idea of the right people: "Those who are productively neurotic, those who are *self*-motivated and *self*-disciplined, those who wake up every day, compulsively driven to do the best they can because it is simply part of their DNA" (2005, p. 15).

Collins calls this the "First Who" principle. It is first about the "who," not the "what," particularly in organizations like ours. Collins says, "In the social sectors, when big incentives (or compensation at all, in the case of volunteers) are simply not possible, the First Who principle becomes even more important. Lack of resources is no excuse for lack of rigor—it makes selectivity all the more vital" (2005, p. 15).

Get the Right People into the Right Seats

This can mean that the wrong people need to get off the bus. Sometimes (though not that often, if it's clear which direction the bus is moving) they need to be shown their stop. Your most important coaching call will be featuring the right players at the right time in the right positions.

Take a look at the organizational chart of your development office. Does it make sense? Does it reflect a strong management team? Does it feature the core "sales team" with other positions supporting that group? Does it reflect your "game plan" with key players and teams aligned with key strategies? Or does it resemble an octopus, with tentacles trying to find roles for players in special circumstances or giving form to the new strategy of the year?

For a bus that makes sense, start with your overall strategy, be clear about it and committed to it, and build and align your team around it.

Give Development Officers a Territory to Call Their Own

We assign each of our major-gift officers a geographic territory that he or she owns and builds strategy around, and in which the officer can develop and sustain relationships. The officers facilitate connections among those relationships that will advance the whole enterprise. We do not assign them certain "gift levels," campaign projects, or methods of giving such as annual, planned, or major. Why not? Because these are not things they can own and develop, and they do not reflect the way donors think. Many of these things have become professional silos, to the detriment of our institutions.

At Colorado College, we ask officers to lead according to their territories and relationship portfolio. They are also silo-busting leaders on campus. They have full access to college trustees and everyone else in their territory. This is why we call them all directors of development. They are raising money, not managing a staff, process, or project. In their presentations, they are asking for three commensurate commitments: an annual one (usually made from income), a legacy one based on estate planning, and a major or leadership one (often made from assets).

Use "Team Selling"

"We were loving our job yesterday in a big way!" This is the sign-off line on an email I received recently from two of our development directors who had just visited a man who was a trustee ten years ago but had since disconnected from the college. He has houses in each of their territories, so they decided to visit him together. They had a wonderful meeting. He received the presentation of the campaign, committed a major gift, and initiated a discussion of more to come. A few weeks later, he came to campus, spoke in a class, and made a seven-figure commitment.

Road warriors can end up working a lonely trail. Making visits with other team members and with managers and leaders is a great opportunity for mutual coaching, idea sharing, information gathering, strategy development, and celebrating victories and losses. As vice president, I regularly make calls with all of our directors of development, as does their direct supervisor, the chief development officer. (They make visits with the president often, of course, and they enjoy that, but this is different; he's sort of the team owner, the big leader, not the coach.) I think the visits they enjoy the most are those they do with each other, and they come back to us and advocate that it is effective and helpful for them to do so.

Act or Ask

This is a great team principle. Everyone on the team should be free to act or ask. Live by this principle, and you will create a culture of action and speed. An internal sense of urgency creates an external sense of urgency: the time is *now*.

I mentioned we have a "just ask" culture. This is a big idea for us. When in doubt, ask. It is an answer to all of these questions and issues you might have heard from your development officers: "What should be the strategy?" Ask. "They haven't given." Have they been asked? "They aren't ready to be asked." How do you know if you have not asked? When are they going to let you know they would like to be asked? What do you think they are expecting if they are not expecting to be asked? Most of our alumni, parents, and other loyal friends very much want to be asked to help in a way that is commensurate with their ability to do so.

Here's a corollary to "act or ask": *hope is not a strategy*.

No More Silos

Seriously. Silo busting means changing how we think about our institutions and how we work. Advancement professionals are great silo busters, because they are naturally and functionally what organizational behaviorists call "boundary spanners," individuals who link their organizations or subunits to external sources of information (see Tushman and Scanlan, 1981, for an example of a seminal article). Most donors, prospective students, parents, and others outside our colleges and universities expect everyone at the institution to be boundary spanners. They think of our institutions as one community, an identifiable whole. Sometimes, it seems they expect all of us to know what all the rest of us are doing! Although this might be unrealistic, our organizations take a leap if we can regularly transcend the traditional barriers between the functions of our colleges and universities. Outsiders don't care much about the differences among the admissions, alumni relations, and financial aid offices. They expect to have one seamless, rich, mutually caring relationship with their institution from first contact to bequest.

One practical application on Colorado College's campus has been a strategic program we call "City Champions." We ask alumni, parents, and other champions throughout the country to help us advance all aspects of the college, not solely in the silos of development, alumni relations, admissions and recruiting, internships, media effort, and so forth. This is messy. It requires a lot of communication across traditional silos on campus and lots of coordination on our part, but we've learned that as we executed this becomes the new way of business.

It's All About Relationships

We know this about the fundraising process. Good fundraisers are great relationship builders. So why do we often forget this principle when it comes to our development teams? We must always think about the whole person when we are working with our staff.

A couple of years ago, one of our officers found her life partner. We celebrated that! The wrinkle was that her partner was well established in her own career and community a five-hour drive from campus. Our officer, who had determined that she was going to move and leave her job at the college, summoned the courage to "just ask" us if we would try letting her live out of her new community, fly out of a different airport to her territories, and visit campus regularly. Her leaders and managers agreed and, perhaps most important, her teammates supported her. So far the experiment is working well. We kept a valuable member on our team who is now even more motivated and grateful.

It is not about money and titles, or even management responsibility. Good development officers will turn down considerably more money from other places to stay with you because they balance many quality-of-life factors in making decisions about their future. One of our development officers has actually put dollar figures on all of the quality-of-life factors important to him. When he totals it up, he is getting quite a nice paycheck! (Certainly, this is not to say we should not pay competitive salaries for development officers or anyone else—only that monetary compensation alone is not enough.)

In creating such an environment, you create a recruiting magnet as well. Word gets out and is reinforced through the recruiting and interviewing process. Word gets out either way. If you are having trouble recruiting good people, look first at your team environment before your pay scale and recruiting strategy.

Dropping Balls

I don't think any of my staff have learned to ride a unicycle (though one of our trustees is working on it). A few of them have learned to juggle—another adventure we have enjoyed in retreat settings, inspired by Michael Gelb's *More Balls Than Hands: Juggling Your Way to Success by Learning to Love Your Mistakes* (2003). It turns out that the key to juggling is the toss, not the catch. You have to be willing to let go and drop balls to learn to juggle.

More important, we have learned a great deal together about how to develop our professional skills and use them to advance the college's mission. We are "loving our jobs in a big way!" Winston Churchill said, "Success is going from failure to failure without losing enthusiasm."

References

Collins, J. *Good to Great: Why Some Companies Make the Leap . . . and Others Don't.* Boulder, Colo.: Jim Collins, 2001.

Gelb, M. J. *More Balls Than Hands: Juggling Your Way to Success by Learning to Love Your Mistakes.* New York: Prentice Hall/Penguin Group, 2003.

Suddes, T. *Take a Quantum Leap: A For-Impact Campaign Manifesto.* For Impact/The Suddes Group, 2006.

Tushman, M. L., and Scanlan, T. J. "Characteristics and External Orientations of Boundary Spanning Individuals." *Academy of Management Journal,* 1981, 24(1), 83–98.

STEVEN D. ELDER *is the vice president for advancement at Colorado College.*

INDEX

NEW DIRECTIONS FOR HIGHER EDUCATION

ORDER FORM SUBSCRIPTION AND SINGLE ISSUES

DISCOUNTED BACK ISSUES:

Use this form to receive 20% off all back issues of *New Directions for Higher Education*.
All single issues priced at **$23.20** (normally $29.00)

TITLE	ISSUE NO.	ISBN
_____	_____	_____
_____	_____	_____
_____	_____	_____

Call 888-378-2537 or see mailing instructions below. When calling, mention the promotional code JBXND to receive your discount. For a complete list of issues, please visit www.josseybass.com/go/ndhe

SUBSCRIPTIONS: (1 YEAR, 4 ISSUES)

☐ New Order   ☐ Renewal

U.S.	☐ Individual: $89	☐ Institutional: $244
CANADA/MEXICO	☐ Individual: $89	☐ Institutional: $284
ALL OTHERS	☐ Individual: $113	☐ Institutional: $318

Call 888-378-2537 or see mailing and pricing instructions below.
Online subscriptions are available at www.interscience.wiley.com

ORDER TOTALS:

Issue / Subscription Amount: $ _____

Shipping Amount: $ _____
(for single issues only – subscription prices include shipping)

Total Amount: $ _____

SHIPPING CHARGES:		
SURFACE	**DOMESTIC**	**CANADIAN**
First Item	$5.00	$6.00
Each Add'l Item	$3.00	$1.50

(No sales tax for U.S. subscriptions. Canadian residents, add GST for subscription orders. Individual rate subscriptions must be paid by personal check or credit card. Individual rate subscriptions may not be resold as library copies.)

BILLING & SHIPPING INFORMATION:

☐ **PAYMENT ENCLOSED:** *(U.S. check or money order only. All payments must be in U.S. dollars.)*

☐ **CREDIT CARD:** ☐ VISA ☐ MC ☐ AMEX

Card number _____ Exp. Date _____

Card Holder Name _____ Card Issue # *(required)* _____

Signature _____ Day Phone _____

☐ **BILL ME:** *(U.S. institutional orders only. Purchase order required.)*

Purchase order # _____
Federal Tax ID 13559302 • GST 89102-8052

Name _____

Address _____

Phone _____ E-mail _____

Copy or detach page and send to: **John Wiley & Sons, PTSC, 5th Floor**
989 Market Street, San Francisco, CA 94103-1741

Order Form can also be faxed to: **888-481-2665**

PROMO JBXND